BAYLES MACK

A Life in Politics, Business, and the Law

LeAnne Burnett Morse

Foreward by The Honorable John L. Napier

Best wishes to my friend
Patrick Arway!!! "The Computer
Man"
          Hope you enjoy!!
                    Bayles

12/23/24

BLUESTOCKING BOOKS

Published by Bluestocking Books.

Bluestocking Books is an imprint of Bluestocking Media, LLC. Fort Mill, South Carolina.

Library of Congress Control Number: 2022913750

ISBN 978-0-9966415-2-4
ISBN 978-0-9966415-3-1 (ebook)

Cover design & interior formatting: Mark Thomas / Coverness.com

For my family and friends, the heart of my story.

Bayles Mack

For Wyatt

LeAnne Burnett Morse

Contents

FOREWORD

Bayles Mack's name is interwoven in the modern history of South Carolina. He has influenced the course our state has taken for well over half a century. For decades Bayles Mack has been a consummate insider in South Carolina.

Two legitimate and compelling questions for a serious student of modern South Carolina public affairs and history should include "What do we need to know about Bayles Mack to learn more about who we are?" and "How has Bayles Mack influenced our history?"

There are, of course, any number of ways we can approach, record, and study the body of thought we call history. It may be the study of movements. It may be a study of the culture embodied in architecture, literature, music, science. Wars. Economics. Events. Politics. Personalities.

My first college history professor concluded his initial lecture by suggesting that a study of personal biography is the most interesting and potentially the most insightful. It enfolds all of the above and gives a human flavor to this confluence of events, people, and places that make history.

This human aspect is immensely important in grasping the full measure of history. To understand the makeup of South Carolina toward the end of the twentieth century and during the first decades of the twenty-first, one must understand the "behind the scenes" figures who have made the system work and the unique relationships they have experienced. This is precisely what Ms. LeAnne Burnett Morse accomplishes in *Bayles Mack: A Life in Business, Politics, and the Law.*

This book spawns a gnawing question for one interested in all the various activities that interact to make up what we ultimately gather from the disorganized mass of historical information. Just think about how much richer our cultural and political understandings are when we have substantial and organized biographical profiles of the men and women, many of whom operate behind the scenes, to support those who happen to emerge in the headlines.

During the course of examining any epoch there are a number of courses one can take. One is to look at the headlines in the print media, and in most recent memory, to review the Google headlines assembled in the electronic media. This approach generally highlights those on the front lines. Another is to look at derivative interpretations, such as articles and news commentaries, which often gloss over and miss personal aspects of relationships in shaping events. Another approach is to delve behind the scenes to see how and why the protagonists interact the way they do. Who really are the personalities that help shape events? Why do people act and react as they do as we compile this mix called history?

One inquiry is equally important to the other. Headlines and press releases are valuable for assessing the temper of the times, but there is more to defining this phenomenon than just the surface events. It is a mixture of the personalities of the players involved in the decision-making combined with an examination of the interaction of these personalities in light of the ambiances surrounding them that make history interesting and cohesive. A balance of all these factors gives us the needed perspective with which to understand the complete picture. It is best called a "special flavor of the times" that only delving into personality can bring to bear. This aspect gets us beyond what otherwise is a sterile accounting of events.

In this probing biography Ms. Morse does just this by capturing the extraordinary career and personality of Bayles Mack. She does this by recounting his interactions with other personalities, politics, and public policy in South Carolina, drawing on his decades of public and personal service.

I first came to know the name Bayles Mack when I was a young legislative assistant to US Senator Strom Thurmond in the 1970s and later as an attorney in private practice when I returned to the state to practice with a Bennettsville law firm. Bayles and I had both graduated from Davidson College near Charlotte, a small college that has a cohesive base of alumni. Thus, Bayles's name came up often and his exploits were of particular interest to me. Never mind that he was in the neighboring congressional district a hundred miles away; it seemed everybody who knew how Columbia and Washington ticked had a story about Bayles Mack. Early in his career he had become the man to know, a "larger than life" figure.

The Mack family is rich in the legal lore of York County, South Carolina, and the nation. Bayles's grandfather was the founding editor-in-chief of *Corpus Juris* and *Corpus Juris Secundum*, the acknowledged encyclopedic references in the whole of American law. His journey to the center of South Carolina's power structure was natural. It came through his family heritage and began in earnest upon his discharge from the military and his apprenticeship with Mr. John Spratt Sr.,

Congressman John Spratt's father. The elder Mr. Spratt became an early mentor. This involvement was in significant legal, financial, and land interests in Fort Mill and in the development and "take-off" of this area as it has tracked the phenomenal growth of Charlotte and the spillover into central South Carolina.

It was almost immediate that Bayles's political genius was recognized, and Congressman Tom Gettys asked him to be his administrative assistant (now generally known as "chief of staff") in Washington. Thus began the axis of tremendously influential activity among Bayles's bases in Washington, Columbia, and his extensive network throughout the state for his skills at problem-solving and behind-the-scenes leadership.

Upon Congressman Gettys's retirement in 1974, there was a substantial interest in a "Mack for Congress" candidacy. Bayles, however, demurred. He decided to stay in South Carolina and focus on politics at the local and state levels. He turned his attention to positions in York County and Columbia, where his service on the South Carolina Highway Commission (now South Carolina Department of Transportation) became legendary.

Bayles's career has tracked South Carolina's movement from a one-party-dominated state to two-party politics. His relationships with Governors Bob McNair and John West led to ties to the heart of establishment politics. His demeanor and temperament have enabled him to be a bridge between various factions in the state whatever the venue and wherever he has been called to serve.

In later years of his service on the highway commission, I witnessed this firsthand when Don Fowler, formerly chair of the Democratic National Committee, and I jointly represented SCDOT in its federal governmental affairs. While representing different political viewpoints,

Don and I marveled at Bayles's talent to command collegiality, comity, and cooperation. I suspect Don would be writing much the same if he were alive today.

South Carolina has long been considered a state dominated by the legislature and boards and commissions. The old highway commission and the evolving transportation commission have always had strong members. Indeed, along with the South Carolina Ports Authority and the boards at the University of South Carolina and Clemson, these appointments have been the crown jewels of delegated power in the state representing both stature and influence.

Watching Bayles as an agent for pulling together the various factions on any matter has been to observe a masterful facilitator and mediator at his best. His diligent work and leadership with Director Elizabeth Mabry and Chairs Morgan Martin, Tee Hooper, and Buck Limehouse, plus long-time commissioners such as Marion Carnell, Bob Harrell, John Hardee, and John M. "Moot" Truluck, were highly instrumental in bringing the commission to consensus on direction and to the point of fruition for two of the major infrastructure landmarks in the state's history: the Ravenel Bridge in Charleston, and the I-77 connection between Columbia and Charlotte.

Bayles's conversations with Senator Thurmond and Senator Hollings were crucial to pave the way for their support on any number of projects critical to the state. He had been Congressman John Spratt's campaign manager and thus had his ear, as well as others in the delegation. He was close to his county neighbor, Governor Jim Hodges, and to Governor Hodges's predecessors and successors. I submit that the collegial interaction between Bayles and his fellow commissioners and Director Mabry led to a high-water mark in SCDOT's federal/ state relationships. No history of highways, transportation, and infrastructure in South Carolina is complete without recognizing and acknowledging Bayles's substantial contributions and steadfast leadership.

By personality and training the Bayles Mack style is one of gentle persuasion. He is firm in his resolve, but he is never one to burn bridges or to be unnecessarily confrontational. I believe this is how he has accomplished so much as a businessman, politician, and lawyer to the powerful and advocate for the less fortunate. My former law partner, state Circuit Court Judge Edward B. Cottingham, a man who held court all over the state, was a good friend of Bayles. He once described Bayles to me by saying, "He is a wise owl, a masterful lawyer; he never puts himself in a position where his adversaries can comfortably tell him no." I also heard Davis Heniford, one of South Carolina's banking and real estate leaders who served with Bayles in a number of sensitive infrastructure assignments, make a similar comment. He said Bayles has a unique ability to gauge how to time public policy decisions.

I have discussed this sense of time and place with Bayles. I believe it derives from his family allegiance to the law and his ancestral tie to the founder of *Corpus Juris,* his love of history and sense of time and place learned at Davidson, and his early tutelage under the elder Mr. Spratt. Whatever the source, it has given Bayles a charisma that he has used over the years to better his community, his state, and his nation.

One of the most revealing attributes about his life has been his ability to evolve with the times yet remain true to his values and convictions. This has enabled him to work across party lines to forge realistic solutions for what others have considered unsolvable problems. During the latter part of the 1900s and up until today, in addition to designing and implementing normal yet complex economic development models, Bayles has been highly instrumental in expanding professional sports development in South Carolina from its base in Charlotte. This derives from Bayles's lifetime interest in consummately crafting relationships with the banking, business, and sports communities in both Carolinas. I have heard it said of Bayles often that he thrives on friendships and relationships. This continued presence in the dynamic growth of the central Piedmont is not only just another case in point to establish his unique place in modern-day South Carolina leadership, but it is also to cement him as one of our critical leaders over decades.

The setting of his unique office in Fort Mill reveals a lot of the Bayles Mack story. It is a refurbished railroad car rich in historical artifacts from which he "conducts" his business and guides his clients. Outside the office setting he is renowned on the dance floor as a world-class shagger and a spiffy dresser who is the envy of all.

Always of good cheer and good humor, he sometimes likes to give the impression of being somewhat of a rascal, but overarching all of this is the simple truth that a deep sense of propriety and purpose governs his life. This makes for a combination that is hard to compete against in the courtroom, the boardroom, or any room Bayles may enter.

Ms. Morse's biography captures the Bayles Mack I know and respect. It depicts the Bayles Mack that history should know. It describes a man from whom professional and amateur historians can learn. This work centers on a man of vision who brings people together. A smart man. A savvy operator. A gracious and generous man. A gentleman. Above all, a good man.

I heartily commend this portrait as indispensable in understanding the temper of the times in South Carolina in the latter part of the twentieth century and the first part of the twenty-first. Without understanding how a man of influence like Bayles Mack shapes business, politics, and policy, one cannot fully understand the keys necessary to unlock the history of the period. But indeed, with an understanding of how Bayles has deployed his many talents and has given flavor to all he does, both professionally and personally, one can then more thoroughly enjoy and appreciate the rich history of our state.

—John L. Napier

John L. Napier is an attorney and formerly a United States congressman from South Carolina and federal judge on the United States Court of Federal Claims in Washington, D.C.

PROLOGUE

I'm not a lawyer's lawyer. Not one lawyer would call me to find out what the real law is. But when there is something tough, they send it to me, because they know I'll make it happen.

—Bayles Mack

The mood on the convention floor each night was nearly as tense as the one outside the barricades surrounding the venue. Warring factions of protestors in the streets garnered headlines on evening news, but the battles going on in the upscale hotels and in official meeting rooms around town, while less physically threatening, were no less volatile. The cult of personality was struggling, having unexpectedly found itself without a headliner candidate, though his storied name was still on everyone's lips. The political vacuum brought the names of previously untapped favorite sons to the forefront as what had looked to some to be a foregone conclusion eleven weeks earlier had turned into a race for the top spot in a suddenly crowded field. The names of candidates barely of electable age were bandied about along with state governors whose political experience was less important than where they came from on the prickly map of electoral math.

Outside, the police tried to keep the increasing protests to a slow burn, while inside, the subtle art of politics gave way to strong-arm tactics as fears of faithless electors and a resulting ticket that couldn't be counted on to make two hundred seventy on the electoral map in November contributed to the chaotic atmosphere. A sense of anticipation for something unknown permeated the air as young delegates weighed the benefits of taking a symbolic stand against the establishment in the same way the exploding culture at large was doing on the evening news. Party leaders worried the youth element might not be easily controlled, and the term "unit rule" formed the basis of the rumors circulating among the delegations. With the convention marching toward its moment of truth, culture and politics erupted in front of millions of stunned Americans watching on television.

On August 28, 1968, the simmering protests over the US government's handling of the Vietnam War tipped the delicate balance into full-scale rioting. And inside the Palmer House Hotel, the South Carolina delegation waited to hear if their governor, himself nursing a growing following as a potential candidate for the vice-presidential nomination, would make good on his threat to unseat them at the eleventh hour and replace them with delegates who would do his bidding. In the midst of this chaos, a thirty-three-year-old delegate watched and waited along with his compatriots to find out if they would be allowed to cast their votes. Two or three of them were part of a larger informal group of eight young politicos who had been staunch Kennedy-ites, and an unexpected change by the Democratic National Committee at the beginning of the convention left the door wide open for them to vote their consciences instead of adhering to the majority-takes-all unit rule. Secretly viewing themselves as the "Vigilante 8," they considered themselves frontline soldiers for Kennedy in the South.

The two or three who were part of the actual delegation saw a chance to express their loyalty with a first-round vote for Edward "Teddy" Kennedy, the younger brother of presumptive nominee Robert F. Kennedy, who had been shot dead in a hotel kitchen some two months earlier. This vote wouldn't look good for their governor, Bob McNair, and his hopes of being chosen as Hubert Humphrey's running mate. No, McNair wanted to deliver South Carolina unanimously for Humphrey on the first vote, and these young turks were interfering with his ambition. They included up-and-coming young men, all ambitious and possessing of the kind of eagerness and unspoiled idealism that is common to political youth who haven't been involved in the game long enough to have the optimism beaten out of them by the cold reality that politics is, at its core, a blood sport.

For one of them, Bayles Mack of Fort Mill, a few years operating in local and state politics had provided enough of a primer to help him gauge the tone of the room and recognize the moment when one had to decide if the issue at hand was a hill worth dying on. It was an ability to read others that would serve him well through a lifelong law practice and a career as a power broker behind the scenes of the political world rather than on its stage. He would be the person candidates called when they needed to get the word out, raise the money, or frame the message to fit the race. From a single admonition by his father to "follow the money," he would steer projects that would bring economic vitality to South Carolina through a series of stepping stones and old-fashioned Southern politicking. Every experience was a learning opportunity for what would be coming down the road, and all the experiences built one upon the other to increase his influence statewide. But all that was still in the formative stages—possibly none more formative than the powder keg he was navigating with his fellow delegates in a tension-filled hotel room.

While famed mayor Richard Daley's city of Chicago blew up outside, the delegate Mack and his like-minded young Democratic idealists learned their first lessons in *national* politics. This son and grandson of lawyers, merchants, and Presbyterian clergy whose family names— Mack, Mills, and Ardrey—featured prominently in history books of the region he called home; this grandson of wealth and scion of a father known for his excesses and a mother known for her forbearance toward her lovable rouge husband and her commitment to her only son, was himself fashioning a life at the confluence of the law, politics, and business. The delegate would retain a lifelong loyalty to his small-town roots and never forget his mother's admonition to "always try to do the right thing; help others and it will be returned," though he would occasionally be the subject of rumors that he didn't tread that path as carefully as she intended. He would draw on his memories of a summer job at the local textile mill, the Saturday shoppers in his uncle's hardware store on Main Street, and the example of community-wide benevolence he witnessed by the town's richest man in choosing which cause or which horse to back all of his political career.

But in that summer of discontent in a city under siege as he waited for a resolution to the delegation crisis, he knew only one thing for sure—influence is a powerful, powerful thing.

4

THE DIRTY HOUSE

The childhood shows the man,
as morning shows the day.

—John Milton

Before he was at the center of political intrigue on a national level, Barron Bayles Mack was a boy like any other of his time living in the rural South. Born September 19, 1934, to a mother he would revere his entire life and a sometimes-absentee father of wealth and privilege, Bayles arrived in a world where the name "Mack" already meant something. His first three years were spent in a house on Clebourne Street in Fort Mill, where his earliest snippets of memory are of playing in the front yard near the porch, where he could look under and see the underpinnings of the house itself. They could also be glimpsed through the floorboards from inside the house. The foundation was not enclosed and chickens wandered about in the shaded area. The sight of the chickens, log footers, and bare earth to an inquisitive little boy would cause him to forever after refer to it as "the dirty house." He was too young to understand his surroundings—too young to be either impressed or ashamed by any kind of house at all, "dirty" or not. But his reaction to the patch of ground where he lived his earliest days foreshadowed an inherent gift that would factor into his later life, both in and out of politics—the ability to see what lies underneath and to call it as he saw it.

Clebourne Street wraps around the upper corner of the historic district in Fort Mill until it joins Tom Hall Street at the top of Main. Thomas Lee Hall was a Fort Mill son who gave his life in service to his country on a French battlefield during World War I. He was awarded the Medal of Honor in recognition of his service and sacrifice, and the town made sure his name would not be forgotten by memorializing it on one of its most prominent streets. It was a fitting tribute to Hall and a progressive step forward for a town that had previously called that stretch of road "Booth Street." The story goes that it had originally been named in honor of John Wilkes Booth after the Civil War. Whether a true story or not, it is not an unbelievable one. The Fort Mill of the late nineteenth and early twentieth century was a decidedly Southern place, though mostly by way of genteel pursuits and a benign nod toward small-town Americana.

When Bayles was growing up, there were four main occupations in the town for putting food on the table. A majority of the town's population of 4,400 worked in one of two textile mills and those who didn't live by the schedule of the mill's steam whistle were likely merchants, cotton farmers, or domestics. Sprinkle in a handful of teachers and another of preachers and that was generally the way of it. It was the need for a preacher that brought the first of the Macks to

Fort Mill. Bayles's grandparents J. B. and Harriet Hudson Banks Mack would heed the pastoral call and in turn introduce both Mack and Banks to the town's rolls of influential families.

Before young Bayles turned four, "the dirty house" was a thing of the past. His father moved the family to a new house he had had built on land he bought from his uncle Edward. Edward had been given the land by his mother, Harriet Banks Mack, Bayles's grandmother. It was just a stone's throw down the street from the Mack homeplace where Bayles spent a lot of his childhood visiting with his grandmother. His grandparents' house, the same one where his own christening would take place, was built in 1871 and once belonged to Harriet's brother before it was bought by her husband, J. B. Mack. It was an impressive two-story structure with tall windows and wraparound porches to capture the refreshing breezes. But unlike most shaded piazzas, this one had a distinctive element that made it stand out from other gracious homes about town—one that made it a place young Bayles loved to play under his grandmother's watchful eye. The house had originally been only a single story. J. B. and Harriet enlarged the house and added the second story and the columned porches in 1910. To one hapless carpenter's misfortune, Harriet was home when he went for the front lawn's mature and shady hickory tree with his saw. It was in the way of the porch, he told her.

"Build the porch around it," she instructed him.

He soon found out Mrs. Mack was not kidding and she wasn't backing down. The carpenter might go, but the tree would stay. The porch was built, and for seventy-nine years locals marveled at the house with the tree growing up through the porch until Hurricane Hugo toppled it in 1989. It took the wind forces of a category-four hurricane to get Harriet's tree. During Bayles's childhood Harriet would sit out on the porch with him while he played with his toys beside the tree's enclosed trunk. Even the local newspaper couldn't resist publishing a charming photo showing three-year-old Bayles in short pants standing on a bench beside the tree holding a toy saw as if he were about to cut it down. Harriet, age ninety-three, is beside him on the bench, smiling for the camera in the way grandmothers are prone to do when their little ones get into something adorably precocious.

J. B. and Harriet had ended up in the house with the porch tree as a result of J. B.'s call to ministry years before. Like many of the earliest settlers to the Carolina Piedmont, which includes Fort Mill in South Carolina as well as neighboring city Charlotte in North Carolina, the Macks had their roots in the auld sod. The town's original settlement, called Little York, was made up of Scots-Irish settlers who could trace their lineage to sympathies with both the House of York and the House of Lancaster. When they set about carving a village from the untouched wilderness, they set up the first house of worship and called it "Unity" as an outward sign of their intention to leave behind old grudges and start fresh in this new place.

It was to this congregation that J. B. Mack came to Fort Mill to serve as pastor a century later.

THE PREACHER

*I have a splendid place here—a good house and over
20 acres of land, garden, and orchard, and everything
necessary.*

—Joseph Bingham Mack

There are not many surviving photographs of Joseph Bingham Mack, but an inspection of those that remain reveal quite a handsome man with a determined set to his countenance. His heavy brow and resolute expression suggest a man who knows his mind and is firm in his convictions. Rather than the soft and somewhat forlorn images of his contemporaries, he looks like a modern man in an old-timey photograph, so familiar is his appearance to our modern eyes. It may be an expression forged as a man of the cloth tempered by war service or the authoritative demeanor of a father of eleven children living in a difficult time in history, but this first Mack to arrive in Fort Mill provided a fitting foundation for a family that would become part of the warp and weft of the fabric of the town.

Born to William and Elizabeth Scoville Bingham Mack in Rochester, New York, on Christmas Eve 1838, J. B., as he was known, moved with his family to Tennessee as an infant. By the mid-1840s they had settled in Columbia, Tennessee, sixty miles southwest of Nashville. He earned his bachelor's degree at the age of fifteen from local Jackson College, where his father had previously served as president. During school he took an apprenticeship with a carriage builder. After graduation he met Dutch portrait painter Joseph H. Van Stavoren, who was beginning to work in a new photography process known as daguerreotype. J. B. traveled with him displaying the new technology in small towns.

In one of the towns J. B. took a break and visited a revival service. It was during this service that he felt his life's call to ministry and soon returned from his travels to continue his education. He went on to complete his studies at Columbia Theological Seminary just as cavalry and cannon took to their battlefields in the Civil War. Following his ordination in 1862 by the Harmony Presbytery of the Synod of South Carolina, he became a regimental chaplain for the 55th Tennessee Infantry. His unit was eventually consolidated with another and he completed his service with the 44th Tennessee Infantry Regiment, ultimately serving under General Joseph E. Johnston of the Army of the Tennessee during the Georgia Campaign in 1864. At the end of his enlistment he returned to serve his presbytery in Mayesville, South Carolina. In due time he met the daughter of another pastor and fellow graduate of Columbia Theological Seminary.

Of Scottish descent, Harriet Hudson Banks was born to William and Mary Elvira Ernestine Harrington Banks in Sumter County, South

Carolina, July 30, 1845. In addition to his longtime pastoral career, William was also active on the Board of Trustees for Davidson College in North Carolina. His devotion to the college would be magnified in the work of his son, schoolmaster Alexander Robinson (A. R.) Banks, Harriet's only sibling. Both of the Banks children would find their way to Fort Mill—Harriet as the wife of J. B. Mack, and A. R. as the master of the town's first school, Fort Mill Academy. All his career he would steer students to higher education at Davidson, strengthening a family commitment to the institution that continues to the current generation. Young Bayles would matriculate at Davidson and carry his time there close to his heart throughout his life.

J. B. Mack and Harriet Hudson Banks were married in Chester County December 15, 1864, in the waning days of the war. They were quickly blessed with children: the first-born, William (1865–1941), whom they called "Willie," was born just ten months after they were wed. Ten more children followed throughout the years, born in various towns in North and South Carolina as J. B.'s pastoral calling took the family from church to church. The next to arrive was Alexander (1867–1906), followed by Edward (1868–date of death unknown), Joseph (1870–1871), Elizabeth (1871–1962), Mary (1872–1962), Harrington (1874–1957), Cornelia (January 1879–June 1879), Luther (1885–1886), Francis "Murray" (1889–1979), and Paul (1894–1897). Of the four children who died in early childhood, infant Luther Bingham Mack was the first to be born in Fort Mill after the family settled there when J. B. became pastor at Unity Church. This posting in Fort Mill allowed them to finally establish roots that would last for generations.

By the time J. B. took over as pastor at Unity Church, he had been a military chaplain in the Confederate service and had also spent four years leading a congregation at Rocky River Presbyterian Church in Concord, North Carolina. But between his military service in Alabama and Georgia and his church in North Carolina, J. B. had a unique opportunity to serve in a way many white pastors in the time of Reconstruction would have been hard pressed to agree to. The port city of Charleston was known as "the cradle of secession." From its shaded piazzas along East Battery Street, indignant residents, alongside the freshly minted Confederate Army's top general, Pierre Gustave Toutant Beauregard, watched the bombardment of Fort Sumter on April 12, 1861. It had been a mere four months since South Carolina became the first state to declare its ties to the United States null and void.

In the four years since US Army Maj. Robert Anderson hauled down the American flag from atop the fort in response to the bombardment, Charleston had turned into a hotbed of rebellion, pitched battles, and blockading ships. Now it stood a smoking ruin. No city in the defeated Confederacy engendered more animosity and cravings for punishment than Charleston. Into this fray came J. B. Mack, newly married and still untested as leader of a large congregation. In Charleston he didn't find one congregation—he found two. Zion Church on Calhoun Street was under the pastoral care of a man who would become a great mentor to J. B. Rev. John Lafayette Girardeau welcomed the assistance of this new pastor and enlisted his help not only with the Zion congregation but also with a second faith community located on nearby Glebe Street. Anyone who has ever visited the city knows it suffers no shortage of churches. They seem to spring from every block, and sister congregations are not uncommon. But the two churches under Rev Girardeau's care differed in that one was a white church and one was home to more than a thousand newly-freed African American congregants. Girardeau dreamed of a unified church and achieved that goal briefly before pressure to maintain separate facilities ended the experiment. However, the separate groups continued to grow and thrive. Over the next few years, J. B. worked alongside Rev. Girardeau ministering to both congregations and the reverend's commitment to the spiritual well-being of those formerly in bondage left a lasting impression on his young assistant.

Nearly 150 years after J. B. and Rev. Girardeau's committed actions in the most difficult period in that city's history, Charleston would see one of its oldest houses of worship desecrated by a racially motivated mass murder that took the lives of nine of the faithful within the walls of their sacred space. The killer, twenty-three-year-old Dylann Roof, had a history of brandishing symbols of his hate, most notably a Confederate battle flag. Emanuel African Methodist Episcopal Church, the site of the massacre, was already standing in Charleston when J. B. and the Reverend walked the city streets ministering to black and white alike. And it stands today, despite Civil War, Reconstruction, the turbulent 1960s, and the murderous rampage of one on whose deaf ears their message of unity and salvation would have surely gone unheeded, then as now.

With the war behind him and his work in Charleston and Rocky River completed, J. B. turned his attention to the congregation at Unity Church in Fort Mill in 1876. He actually pastored two churches at this time, Unity and Waxhaw Church, in nearby Waxhaw, North Carolina. The presbytery paid him a combined salary of $1,500 annually. He and Harriet welcomed their last three children in Fort Mill and made their family home at the corner of the streets known today as Confederate and Banks.

J .B. was Unity's twenty-fifth pastor and began his service in its third sanctuary. In the years since Unity's first house of worship was constructed upon the church's founding in 1788, two wooden structures at two locations had succumbed to fire. This third was in yet another location, built on present-day Tom Hall Street, where Unity still stands. But this particular sanctuary was also built with wood. Upon finding his new church without a bell to call the faithful to worship, J. B. commissioned one from a Baltimore foundry and had it hung in this church, where it stayed for three years until this building too was consumed by fire in 1880. The congregants had built three buildings on three sites and had seen them all rendered to ashes. This time they would do it differently.

The fourth sanctuary, the first in brick, was pleasantly sited on the same gentle rise overlooking present-day Tom Hall Street in the heart of town where the last of the wooden structures had stood. It was dedicated in 1881, with Rev. Mack's bell, undamaged by the previous fire, ringing out the call to worship from its new belfry.

For 136 years the brick church stood, even surviving a devastating hurricane in 1989. But on December 10, 2018, fire again tore a path through Unity Church, starting in the classroom behind the chancel wall. This fourth sanctuary, and its larger modern sister standing adjacent, survived the fire though damage was severe to the 1881 building. But the brick walls the congregants from J.B.'s day built for this purpose stood. And in its belfry a bell still hangs today, bearing this inscription:

Presbyterian Church, Fort Mill, S.C., Rev. J. B. Mack, Pastor
Henry McShane and Company, Baltimore, Md., 1877

J. B. did not remain in the pastor's position at Unity long. He wrote to his father, William Mack, expressing his concern that the presbytery had been falling behind in its payment to him for the combined pastoral position and that he had offered to take a smaller salary. But he had an opportunity to take over a church in Columbia and was weighing his options. Salary wasn't the only consideration on his mind.

> *I have a splendid place here—a good house and over 20 acres of land, garden, and orchard and everything necessary. The school is near and my influence in this section is growing.*[1]

By this time he was serving as Fort Mill Academy's board of trustees chairman, and he felt torn about the possibility of leaving Fort Mill behind.

> *I feel that God sent me here to save the church in [Columbia], to revolutionize our Presbytery, and to vindicate truth and law. But that is done. Is it a sign to leave or not?*[2]

His father, who had been encouraging him to stay where he was, had a change of heart that he expressed in a letter of April 20, 1876.

> *[I] hoped things would work out for you and your family at Fort Mill. Now for some reason, I feel different. If you see your way clear, Go, and the Lord be with you.*[3]

J. B. did decide to move on to the church in Columbia, but he kept the house in Fort Mill, where he and Hattie would one day return. In his final working years he changed course and left the pulpit to lend his assistance in financial management to his seminary alma mater, and later to funding issues for Davidson College, where he served as a trustee. He also wrote and spoke extensively on church matters and was an early investor in Fort Mill Manufacturing Company, which became Springs Cotton Mills and later, Springs Industries. In fact, records show that at one point he was second only to Leroy Springs in the number of shares owned in the company.

J.B. believed Springs, the company's president and son-in-law of company founder Samuel Elliott White, was trying to steal his shares. He wrote of his concerns to his son William, who investigated and replied to his father that Mr. Springs wasn't attempting to steal them but that he was interested in acquiring them for a good price. Springs called it "buying them right." J.B. and some smaller investors sold their shares to him. A surviving letter from J.B. to oldest son William, who was by this time on the verge of his career-making turn in New York, reveals his concerns for the future even as he was pondering the stock sale. The letter, addressed to "Willie" and dated August 15, 1899, refers to the recent drought and resulting poor corn and cotton crops and goes on to address the future.

> "I am getting old. My active work is about over. We have educated six of you by hard self-denial. Murray [the youngest surviving son] must be educated. Your mother must have rest now and comfort. Your Uncle [actually brother, not uncle] Alex's treatment of his mother proves that I must not leave your mother to the mercy of any child. To provide for our old age and to educate Murray is my plan. I have written thus fully as you ought to know the status, and to arrange matters wisely if anything should suddenly happen to Your Father.[4]

J.B. died in Fort Mill on May 24, 1912. He did not live to meet his great-grandson Bayles or see the growing influence of the Mack name in the latter part of the twentieth century. His beloved wife, Harriet, lived on until 1937, however, playing an important role in her grandson Bayles's life.

Thus, the Mack family had its preacher and was established in Fort Mill. From Bayles's mother's side of the family would come the merchants in time. But it was J. B. and Harriet's oldest son, William, who would introduce the family to a new vocational pursuit that would bring with it wealth and prestige. His efforts had perhaps the single most defining impact on the fortunes of the Macks for the next four generations. William wasn't a pastor who preached the Word. He wasn't a merchant or a farmer or a textile baron. He was a scholar and a businessman.

And most importantly, he was a lawyer.

THE LAWYER

*There is no sense in merely being a lawyer unless you are
a good one.*

—William Mack

Bayles Mack is a lawyer. His son is a lawyer. His grandson is a lawyer. And his father was a lawyer. The study and practice of the law seems like it's in the Mack DNA—a birthright of sorts. But where did it come from, this recurring call to the service of Lady Justice? Its origins can be traced back two generations before Bayles would sit for his bar exam.

William Mack, the oldest of J. B. and Harriet's children, did not have the same call to ministry as his father had. Born in Mayesville, South Carolina, on October 24, 1865, he finished his basic schooling early and went to Davidson College, where he graduated at age sixteen. From there the law beckoned and he continued his studies at the University of Missouri. After graduation and passing the Missouri bar, he practiced in Independence, Missouri briefly and was soon recruited by a firm in San Francisco. He spent two years working in California and then turned his attention east to New York City, where he would make his mark and his fortune.

William got to work quickly upon arrival in New York. He began practicing with a new partner, Charles W. Dumont. But it was not the *practice* of law that would etch William's name into history books and bring him considerable wealth; it was actually the books themselves.

When lawyers take on cases, they may have a solid knowledge of particular areas of the law that pertain to the types of cases they regularly handle. But they cannot know the full breadth of legal opinion, especially when it's constantly evolving. Today they can use the Internet to search not only the written laws but also the interpretation of those laws in real court cases. Judicial decisions serve as precedents to alter thereafter the way a law is interpreted, and lawyers need to use those decisions to craft their own cases. Long before the Internet put this vast collection of information at the fingertips of any student or clerk with a computer, attorneys had to rely on multi-volume sets in book form. The resulting work was referred to as a *cyclopedia*. The term indicates a comprehensive reference work relating to one subject as opposed to an *encyclopedia*, which is also a comprehensive reference work but covers a wide range of subjects.

William Mack and Charles Dumont were about to expand their area of expertise. The law partners went into the publishing business. The November 1900 issue of *The American Lawyer* reported that the presentation of a new reference work on American and English law had been announced by a new name in publishing. The work, *The Law Cyclopedia,* "has been put on foot by a new corporation, organized for the purpose, with a capital of $100,000, called the American Law Book Company, whose headquarters and editorial and business offices are in the Equitable Building, No. 120 Broadway, New York."[5]

The piece went on to describe the planned work as thirty-two volumes in length, to be released at a rate of four to six per year. It also reported that Charles W. Dumont was the president of the newly formed company and William Mack would be the work's editor-in-chief. Rather than pulling information from legal digests or the work of other writers reporting on the cases, *The Law Cyclopedia* would feature research exclusively from original sources.

The piece ended with a fairly obvious endorsement stating, "The work will not be done by law students, nor by callow graduates from the law schools, but Mr. Mack has selected an able and competent corps of assistants, who will work on a uniform system under his direction." [6] It was quite a glowing recommendation for work that had not even begun at that point.

It proved to be only the beginning of the company's success. The American Law Book Company would go on to release *Corpus Juris* in 1914 and the updated *Corpus Juris Secundum* in the 1920s.

With their reference works selling to country lawyers and big-city firms alike, the company was extremely profitable. A dozen years after the company's founding, the copyright page in an April 1912 release of a new volume of *Cyclopedia* listed an affiliation with a London publishing company, indicating their work was also being used across the pond. The dedication by William Mack gives a glimpse into what those first twelve years had meant to him.

To

CHARLES WALTER DUMONT

more than to any other man is due the existence of the Cyclopedia
of Law and Procedure. His was the idea; his was the plan; and
his has been the business ability and energetic management, as
organizer and president of The American Law Book Company, which
have made possible the successful publication of these volumes,
which are therefore respectfully dedicated to him.[7]

William Mack

⁎

William was living well on Flatbush Avenue in Brooklyn, but he wasn't enjoying his success all alone. A year before the American Law Book Company saw its name featured in *The American Lawyer*, William had married Minnie Frank Bayles in Port Jefferson, New York. Port Jefferson was Minnie's hometown; she was born there in 1867 and her family owned a successful shipbuilding company in the town. Her father, James, and his brother Charles started the Bayles Shipyard in 1835 and worked both together and separately in the industry for many years. Minnie's brother James Elbert Bayles eventually joined their father in business. It is thought the Bayles yard built more than 140 wooden ships from 1835 until 1917. A list of the names of the vessels reveals several that were named for family members, including the *James E. Bayles*, a 140-foot schooner built in 1874. There is also a listing for a 68-foot schooner named the *Millie Frank,* built in 1870. It's possible the old records erroneously recorded "Millie" instead of "Minnie" and that the vessel was named for his daughter, who was born just three years prior.[8]

Minnie was born February 22, 1867, and married William Mack on June 1, 1899. No stranger to a life of privilege, her life with William was a continuation of wealth and status in the city. Photographs of Minnie reveal a stylish woman of means, including one where she is wearing a fur stole and carrying an enormous hand muff, both made of white winter ermine. A brilliant white with distinctive black "tail tip" marks, this expensive fur was commonly used by European royalty in their ceremonial robes. Only the very rich could afford to warm themselves with ermine. The photographer seems to have captured her in a playful moment in the shot, as she looks into the camera with a look that implies she thinks he might be pulling her leg about something. Another photograph depicts Minnie in an all-white belted confection with puffed sleeves, a bow at the neck, a parasol, and an elaborate hat. Beside her is a well-behaved dog and she's leaning on what looks to be a tree trunk in front of a painted nature scene background. The incongruity of leaning on a tree out of doors in such finery also doesn't seem to be lost on her, given her expression.

William and Minnie had only one child, a son also named William. They gave him Minnie's maiden name as well. William Bayles Mack was born October 20, 1903 in New York. He would grow up to be a very different man than his father. It may have been the result of a natural difference in personality or the fact that he would be raised largely outside of his father's influence and guidance. Whatever the cause, the glamorous New York life would not be for little William. When he was four years old his mother died and the trajectory of his life was changed. Minnie Frank Bayles Mack passed away on February 21, 1908, one day before her 41st birthday. William Sr. was now a widower in a big city with a demanding job, and keeping William with him would have meant the boy would be raised essentially by servants. William Sr. made the decision to send his son to Fort Mill, where he could be raised by his grandparents, J. B. and Harriet Mack.

Whether or not sending him to Minnie's family on Long Island was an option isn't known, but whatever the case, the young master arrived in the small Southern town where he would spend the rest of his life.

William's son Bayles remembers traveling by train to New York once a month to see his grandfather when he was growing up. He remembers that each Christmas they would spend the days prior to the holiday in New York with William Sr. and then take the overnight train home on Christmas Eve, arriving Christmas morning. When they got to their house, Santa had always been there and left his annual trove of gifts and Bayles wondered how he had known to come to Fort Mill when they had been in New York until only that morning. He didn't realize at the time that the family servants, Lucille and Pet Potts, who lived in a separate house on the property and had stayed behind while the family traveled, were responsible for setting up the festive vignette around the tree. Lucille kept house and took care of the family, and Pet was William's chauffeur. It was a very privileged life in a small town where most families did not have wealthy New York grandfathers or domestic help to handle all the logistical details of maintaining the illusion of Santa having stopped by on his trip around the globe.

Young Bayles was in awe of his larger-than-life grandfather and the two grew close. William Sr. was a prolific letter-writer, sometimes writing more than one letter a day to send to Fort Mill. One letter, written to his mother when he was twenty-five years old, praises her for his upbringing.

> *March 1, 1891. Your old-fashioned ideas were taught me*
> *when a baby boy. All your children and their children's*
> *children will be proud that they are descendants of that . . .*
> *old-fashioned Southern school.*[9]

He regularly weighed in on Bayles's young life when writing to William in later years. Many of those letters survive.

> *June 21, 1937. I am not surprised that he [Bayles] wants a dog, but am rather inclined to get him to put it off until he gets into the new house, so that the dog may not be running around from one house to another, thereby disturbing the community.*[10]

The dog in question continued to be a topic in subsequent correspondence.

> *October 11, 1937. I wish Bayles had Roma's [a live-in member of William's household staff] wire-haired terrier. He is a fine dog, particularly as a watch dog, but barks too much for my nerves. However, I guess Bayles is satisfied with his mongrel pup, which seems to be a fine dog and probably might, under proper training, make a good possum dog.*[11]

He concluded that letter, "With my best to the three of you and the pup, Dad." In a second letter that same day he spoke of Bayles's religious education.

> *October 11, 1937. Am glad to hear that the laddie has joined the Sunday-school, and, of course, I am glad that you have chosen the Presbyterian, although the Baptist Sunday-school would have pleased me just as well, for you will remember that your own mother was a Baptist.*[12]

While his letters to his son, William, could be terse and chastising, he showed a softer side when he talked about his grandson.

August 19, 1938. Tell Elizabeth and Bayles that I enjoyed my visit very much indeed and hope that I may see you all again Christmas. Tell Bayles he must be sure to let me know what he wishes Santa Claus to send him for a Christmas present.[13]

This time he ended with the words "With love to the three of you from Grandad."

The next year, in a letter to his daughter-in-law he had a warning for Bayles, who had recently acquired a new toy.

June 1, 1939. Be sure to see that Bayles does not do any damage with his pea shooter. Looking back on my boyhood days, I cannot remember anything more liable to do damage than a pea shooter in a boy's hands. Perhaps if the old score was available it would show thousands of eyes put out by this instrument.[14]

On some occasions his words gave insight to the state of affairs at the time. Referencing President Franklin D. Roosevelt in a letter on April 26, 1939, he wrote,

While I do not agree with the president in all things, I am rather inclined to think he is right when he says the South has become our problem No. 1, at least from an agricultural point of view.[15]

With war raging in Europe, Christmas plans for 1939 were on hold.

September 22, 1939. Tell him [Bayles] not to be disappointed if Uncle Harry and his Grandad do not get to Fort Mill

on Christmas. Things are tightening up quite some in the "present emergency" that is now closing in on our country.[16]

Occasionally William Sr. would demonstrate a wry humor in his letters. Referring to a clipping he was enclosing from the *New York Herald Tribune,* which had been handed to him by the paper's editor, he wrote,

> *December 31, 1937. This paper being a Republican paper, I would not have seen it if the editor had not been so kind. . . . From this you will notice that the Mack family is rapidly infiltrating into the Yankees and other Northern Folks.*[17]

At one point he had occasion to complain about the cost of land in Fort Mill, which had risen to $56 per acre on a tract he had considered buying.

> *March 17, 1939. This is St. Patrick's Day, and I do not believe that the old Saint would have bought land, even without snakes on it, around Fort Mill at $50.00 an acre in 1939.*[18]

William Sr. may have felt it was both his right and his duty to offer advice and instruction to his son's family as he was the one providing the financial support for Bayles and his parents that would allow the life of privilege to continue. Upon William Sr.'s death in 1941, William inherited between four and five million dollars. It was enough, especially in those days, to last them a lifetime with normal stewardship. But William, called "Billee," didn't plan on being a good steward. When Bayles was a bit older, Billee told him bluntly not to expect to inherit anything from him.

"There's the making-it generation and the spending-it generation, son," he told him. "And I'm the spending generation."

Billee was good to his word and he did spend it all. He was generous with others and liked to pick up the tab wherever he went. He also spent a lot of time and money on liquor and could be found buying rounds in the local bars most any night. He was a lawyer by trade himself, but since he didn't have to work, he didn't bother to. When he did practice, he would often do it pro bono. Early on he did provide a small amount that Bayles's mother put into a trust along with some stock to allow their son to go to college. It was that money from his grandfather's estate that would pay Bayles's way through Davidson College. After that, he was on his own.

Grandfather William Mack had been born six months after the end of the Civil War and died December 7, 1941—the day Pearl Harbor was attacked. From horse-and-buggy travel to industrialization and jet airplanes that rained death from the sky—his lifetime spanned a period of tremendous change. Perhaps that would have given him some perspective on the times his grandson would live to see. Either way, it looked as though Bayles would have to be part of "the making-it generation." And he would rise to the challenge, falling back on the example set by his grandfather, the teachings of his maternal grandmother, and the calm and steady guidance of the woman he called his rock: Elizabeth Matilda Mills Mack. Mama.

LIBBA AND HER BILLEE

*She was my rock rather than my dad because my dad
drank too much. You never knew if he was going to
be off the wall somewhere.*

—Bayles Mack

Fort Mill is dotted with historic houses that have ties to the Mack
family in some way, but they don't all come from the Mack side of
the family. If you visit Bayles today in his restored home on Tom
Hall Street, you can take the first few steps up the central staircase
to the first landing and you will find yourself standing in a spot that
is significant to family history. It was on this landing that a double-
ring wedding ceremony was held on November 14, 1900. One of the
couples married that day included the house's owner at that time, E.

W. Kimbrell, and his bride, Myra Adelia Fravor. The other couple was John Barron Mills and Ziza Young. They would have several children, including a daughter they named Elizabeth Matilda, whom everyone called Libba. She would marry William Mack (Billee) and they would have one child, Barron Bayles Mack. The boy would take part of his name from his maternal grandfather, the same John Barron Mills marrying on this staircase, and the other part from Minnie Frank Bayles, the paternal grandmother he never knew. But all that was still in the future when Libba Mills was a girl in Fort Mill growing up the second of eight children. Born May 7, 1904, she joined older brother Ladson and soon welcomed younger brother John Barron (J. B.) Jr. around the time the family moved to their new classical revival style home on Confederate Street. Siblings Ziza, Frances, Evelyn, and the twins, James and Jean, would follow. John Barron Sr. was a cotton broker and the family did well in the formative years of the new century. The Mills family made its living primarily in the merchant trade, owning mercantiles, hardware stores, flower shops, and the like in the area for years to come. In 1930 the grandson of J. B. Mack and the daughter of J. B. Mills were united in marriage and the two families were forever linked.

When Minnie Bayles Mack passed away in New York in 1908 and her husband William sent their son, five-year-old William, to Fort Mill to be raised by his grandparents, Libba Mills was a girl of four. They lived in close proximity and their families were prominent in the small town. It was no surprise that Libba and Billee would travel in the same circles. They were married on July 13, 1930, and soon they moved into what their son Bayles would remember as "the dirty house," where he himself would be born four years later on September 19.

From the beginning, the family dynamic was established. Billee was the man of the house but not the patriarch. That role belonged solidly to his father in New York, William Sr. It was he who provided for the family, allowing for a lifestyle that included domestic help and a driver for Billee so he could spend his time in leisurely pursuits. Often these pursuits ended with him too inebriated to drive, so the arrangement was ideal. Billee lived the life of a wealthy scion while Libba adhered to a more practical and low-key existence. This wasn't New York, after all. In 1937 Billee built the house on Banks Street where the family moved when Bayles was three. Next door to the house itself he built a stand-alone law office, but the practice of law for Billee was more style than substance. This is evident in the way his father rebuked him in letter after letter, year after year.

> *June 21, 1937. Glad to know you are back again at your office, and hope you will make it a regular thing in preparing your cases, acquiring new business, and keeping up with the statutes and decisions of your state.*[19]

> *September 13, 1937. A letter from Uncle Ed [William's brother] indicates that he is perfectly willing to have executed to him, and to execute, quitclaim deeds along the lines detailed to you in a previous letter from me.*
>
> *This being the case, please promptly, and as soon as possible, for his sake and the peace of mind of all of us, execute valid quitclaim deeds from all the heirs.*[20]

October 5, 1937. Please be frank with me. Write at once whether or not you intend to prepare those quitclaim deeds.[21]

October 8, 1937. (Letter to daughter-in-law Elizabeth) P.S. Have not heard from Billee, so I assume that he does not intend to prepare the papers. I have written to him telling him that if he does not intend to do so at once, I shall have to make other arrangements.[22]

October 11, 1937. I have been wholly willing to trust this matter to you, but expected you to act more promptly than you have done. Whatever is necessary to be done should have been started quite a while ago. Some of us, maybe, Ed or myself, or both, may be dead before the transaction is consummated.[23]

October 11, 1937 (second letter that day) As I have not heard from you . . . as to your intention of preparing quitclaim deeds for me, I must cancel your authority.[24]

October 19, 1937 It is difficult to see how you can make even a "stab" at practicing law if you attend to your clients' affairs in the desultory manner you have handled this job.[25]

October 19, 1937. (second letter that day) Tomorrow will be your birthday. Your achievements to date have not been such as to call for congratulations, but maybe you may make tomorrow a birthday date on which you can make a right-about turn toward success. With continued hopes for you, Devotedly, Dad.[26]

*

Billee was described as a real character by everyone who knew him from a young age. All his life he was spoken of with affection, like a truant boy who would show up eventually with an impish grin making it impossible to stay mad at him. In Libba's eyes he could do no wrong. It's not that she didn't see any flaws in him; she just resolved to smooth them over and take up the slack herself. He had followed in his venerated father's footsteps in one regard and become a lawyer. But his career trajectory was almost stalled before he even finished high school. He managed to get himself kicked out of Fort Mill High over an incident with a teacher.

Billee was small in stature and sometimes used his larger-than-life personality to make up for it. A lackadaisical student at best, he had grown bored of the lesson one day and put his head down on his desk. Miss Lana Parks was his teacher and every day she would put ten vocabulary words on the chalkboard and drill the students on spelling them. His fellow pupils reported that when Ms. Parks saw Billee's head on the desk, she tried to engage him and asked him to spell "chrysanthemum." He reportedly looked up and then, without acknowledging her, nonchalantly put his head back down on the desk. The students said she then tapped him on the head with her long nails to get his attention. What he did in response could have landed him in jail. Upon feeling the tapping on his head, he reached and grabbed Ms. Parks by her hair and slammed her head on the desk. He was promptly expelled from school.

His grandfather J. B. Mack had passed away and Grandmother Harriet was raising him on her own. Harriett brooked no tolerance for such behavior and promptly consulted her son (and the boy's father) William in New York. Billee was dutifully shipped off to the Porter Military Academy in Charleston.

The incident at Fort Mill High wasn't the first evidence of a wild streak in Billee. He and his and friends had been known to set up buckets in various places and fill them with explosives. They did it one night at Unity Church, but thankfully there was no damage. A friend's house did not escape unscathed, however. They blew out a number of the windows of that dwelling. Ironically, Billee at one time expressed an interest in attending a theological seminary as had his grandfather. His father, William Sr., discouraged such a course on the basis that he would not make money in the profession, but it's unlikely ministry would have been a good match for Billee's personality and habits anyway. The rigid discipline of Porter Military Academy served to bring him into line and he graduated in 1920. From there he went to college at Washington and Lee in Lexington, Virginia, graduating in 1925. He then went to law school at Cumberland University in Lebanon, Tennessee. His choice of schools was one small act of rebellion, refusing to choose the schools where his own father had been so demonstrably successful.

When he returned to Fort Mill a newly minted attorney, he was the first one in town. He practiced for a while in an office upstairs in the Ardrey building on Main Street and later in the back of local doctor's office before he built the office beside his Banks Street home. His good friend, John Spratt Sr., descendant of Fort Mill's founder, Thomas Spratt, was Billee's contemporary. When they passed the bar, they both returned to York County to practice: Spratt in York and

Billee in Fort Mill. They remained friends and drinking buddies—two wealthy scions with personal chauffeurs who could take them from place to place so they could play much harder than they worked. It was said by people who knew the two that the South Carolina bar was the only one Spratt and Mack ever passed. At all others, the story went, they stopped and stayed a while.

While Billee "practiced" law, Libba saw to the household and to their son, who was showing his own talent for gathering people about himself. He had his father's easy way with people, but his mother was determined he would have purpose and be a good citizen. To this end, she encouraged him to spend time with her mother, Ziza Young Mills. Her father, J. B. Mills, had passed away in 1929. Their home was in close proximity to Main Street and the Mills family had businesses there, so Bayles was a frequent visitor to the stores. When he was eight years old he would go with his grandmother into Martin's Drugstore, where Dr. Martin maintained a section of bins filled with seeds. He would encourage Bayles to reach into the celery seed bin to see how many he could pull out. The tiny seeds would fall through his fingers and he would be left with some stuck to his hands. Dr. Martin would scrape those off into a bag and give them to Bayles to take to his mother for planting.

When Bayles started school at Fort Mill Grammar School, he could look from the front steps of the building right at his grandmother's Confederate Street front porch. He often made his way there when he should have been in class. On the weekends his father would spend his time in the Rexall Pool Hall on Main Street and Bayles would walk the two blocks to his grandmother's house to spend his day with her. (Rexall Drugs across the street complained about their name being used on the pool hall, so the owner got around that issue by changing the spelling to "Rexawl"—a tricky solution that probably wouldn't fly today.) Bayles's grandmother's house was a second home to him. When he wasn't with Grandmother Mills, he could often be found with his great-grandmother Harriet at the house with the tree growing through the porch. It too was located on Confederate Street, the first street in Fort Mill to have pavement. Their house was at the corner of Confederate and Banks Street, so the world Bayles primarily inhabited was a small one between home, church, and his grandparents' houses. But the other end of Banks Street ended where another world entirely began, and from this area Bayles would make friends with his earliest playmates and develop a sense of racial equality that many white children growing up in the South would not be so quick to learn.

The Paradise community of Fort Mill emerged in the early part of the twentieth century as an enclave for African American families. Prior to this, most black families had lived in a handful of neighborhoods scattered around town, typically close to the railroad, where many found employment. When new homes began to crop up several blocks northeast of Main Street, it marked the beginning of a tight-knit community that would also become home to churches and, in 1924, a quality school for the children whose facilities had always been hand-me-down buildings when they were no longer in use for the white population. Legend has it that on washday a couple happened by the neighborhood with their car windows open and remarked on the singing they heard coming from the women tending the week's laundry.

"It sounds like paradise," was the reported evaluation, and the name stuck.

Even today the area around Steele Street and Joe Louis Street is still referred to as "Paradise." Steele and Banks Streets met at Tom Hall

Street, so the Mack house Bayles's father had built for his family when Bayles was three years old was geographically close to Paradise. There existed a perceived gap between the two "sides" of town, or more accurately between the races that lived on each side. The dividing line was Tom Hall Street. But for the Mack family no such barrier existed, and many of Bayles's young friends lived in Paradise. He would walk to their neighborhood, where they would play outside until Bayles had to get home for dinner. In those years all his friends were African American with the exception of one boy who lived on Allison Street, but he wasn't a favorite of Bayles's because they regularly got into fights. By contrast, his relationships with the children in Paradise were collegial, and with their parents he demonstrated what was in that era a noted sign of respect by addressing them as "Uncle" or "Aunt" when he was offered such familiarity. The Macks' progressive attitude toward racial differences was instilled early in Bayles and it informed his relationships throughout his life.

*

With Billee determined to spend every penny William Sr. had left him on himself and others, keeping up the family's lifestyle eventually required assistance from Libba. She found work as a secretary at Springs Cotton Mills working for mill superintendent Lee Skipper, but it wasn't long before the company's president, Elliott White Springs, commandeered her services. The company had been founded by his grandfather, Samuel Elliott White, in 1887 as Fort Mill Manufacturing Company and later run by his father, Leroy Springs. When Elliott inherited the reigns of the company, it was a collection of disparate mills in financial trouble. He consolidated the mills under the name "Springs Cotton Mills" and made them profitable. In fact, Elliott would be responsible for developing a global brand, Springmaid, that would be known the world over for its linens. But being a corporate honcho had not been his dream. In World War I he volunteered early for military service, joining the army. Since America was not yet in the war, he was sent to England to train and fly with the Royal Air Force as a pilot. Later, when America did become involved, he transferred back to the army's Air Service. His combat experience with the RAF had made him a top pilot and he became the nation's fifth ranked flying ace. After his military service he would ever after be called "the Colonel."

He loved adventure and writing and wanted to spend his life engaging in such pursuits. His nod to this early dream for his life that had to be put aside for practical purposes was to continue writing throughout his career. It was in this endeavor that he came to employ Elizabeth Mills Mack.

He poached Lee Skipper's assistant saying, "I need somebody to help me. Lee, you don't need anybody. Elizabeth, you come over and help me while I'm writing my books."

She proved to be invaluable to his work, assisting him by transcribing his written notes and working with him at his executive office and also at his home office at the White Homestead, where she became good friends with his wife, Frances. On Saturdays they also worked on his writing projects in yet a third "office," a restored luxury railcar named the "Loretto," which had originally been built by the Pullman company for U.S. Steel president Charles M. Schwab. It boasted Cuban mahogany paneling, a crystal chandelier, and gold-plated beds, all of which the Colonel maintained. When not in use for travel, he had the car set up on a railroad spur the company owned not far from his house and he liked to work there. Bayles remembered occasionally accompanying his mother to the train car and playing outside while she typed the handwritten manuscripts the Colonel had given her.

If you schedule an appointment to meet with Bayles today, it will take place in one of the most unique spaces in town—a 1946 model, eighty-five-foot, stainless-steel passenger railcar in the fashion of a traditional Pullman, but larger. It sits on permanent rails and has been adapted for use as an office with a unique interior. Aside from his grandfather William's carved partner's desk and a full conference table, the car maintains its private sleeping berth and lavatory. Since 2006 it has been a fixture on Confederate Street, just a block from the house where his Grandmother Mills lived and at the site of the parking lot where his grammar school once sat. The name on the side of the car is emblazoned in large black letters: ELIZABETH MILLS MACK. The car is named for his mother, and his love of trains as well as the idea of using a railcar as an office can all be traced back to her. Even the choice of fabric for the interior wainscoting can be tied to Libba.

In homage to Springs Cotton Mills and the Colonel's train car office where his mother had worked, he decided he wanted to feature a room of the company's memorabilia. He already owned several items such as prints of the famous advertisements that his mother had been given as an employee. He contacted the Colonel's daughter, Anne Springs Close, and asked if he might be able to acquire a few more pieces to add to the collection. Though he knew the family, he still felt a bit sheepish about it appearing that he was trying to copy something the Colonel had done. It was another example of Bayles being afraid of seeming to get above himself. His mother's lessons on humility still resonated and he guarded against showy behavior. He told Ms. Close that he was doing up a train car, "nothing like the spectacular one that your father owned, but just a little something that had been inspired by it. I don't want to be obnoxious about it, but I would like to do it, and my mother would have thought it was great since she worked for your dad. My connection to the trains is through you all."

He remembered that Ms. Close believed many people living in town by that time didn't know about the Colonel. He said she told him, "Nobody knows who Daddy is anymore and maybe this will help revive his name in the town."

An awful lot of people do, in fact, know who Colonel Springs was, although younger people who don't remember the mills may actually come to learn about him because they've heard of his daughter and not the other way around. The Anne Springs Close Greenway takes its name and its mission from her, introducing new generations to the legacy and history of one of Fort Mill's leading families. Colonel Springs was known for his generosity to the people of Fort Mill, and his daughter carries on that same spirit. Besides the items for the display, she also gave him a bolt of original Springs "Persian Print" fabric that had been manufactured in the late 1940s or early 1950s. He used it extensively inside the car as café curtains on the windows and as upholstery for the wainscoting.

In the course of his professional work some years back, Bayles had an opportunity to travel with Springs Industries executives via railcar to their New York office for a meeting, and he dreamed of using his own car for travel on the rails. He soon learned that the price for hooking onto a train going in whatever direction you wanted to go was $8,500 per day. Having the car ride the rails was out of the question, so making it stationary was the next best thing. He had engineers build out the rails it would sit on using concrete "ties" instead of the standard creosote-treated wood so they would not rot. *The Rock Hill*

Herald ran an article on April 24, 2006, titled "Getting His New Office on Track." Photos included with the article show the car once it had been craned into place and was ready for final retrofitting. The York County Regional Chamber of Commerce hosted a ribbon-cutting on May 17. A photo of that event shows a group gathered around Bayles with their hands holding up the ribbon he's preparing to cut. One of the men in the group is smiling and wearing quite a unique sports coat. The man is Elliott Close, grandson of Colonel Springs and one of Anne Springs Close's children. The coat is a one-of-a-kind piece the Colonel had made for himself years ago. It is made entirely of Springs Cotton Mills Persian Print fabric, the same that features so prominently inside the railcar behind them.

*

Whatever anger or disrespect was coursing through Billee in high school that would cause him to assault a teacher was drummed out of him at Porter Military Academy, and the rest of his life he was known as a congenial and generous man. His generosity with finances was a detriment to his family, but he loved being able to play the role of the Southern gentry for whom money is but a coarse subject best not discussed in polite company. To those with money, to be thought to be engaging in the pursuit of or too concerned with preserving such a vulgar commodity was beneath one's dignity. Billee might drink it up or give it away, but he wasn't interested in earning it. Still, Bayles remembered him as "the smartest man I ever knew."

It was a trait that Billee would demonstrate in ways other than being a successful earner and Bayles was his eager pupil. Billee had a natural understanding of people and how they did business. His gregarious personality drew people to him and he made connections easily until it seemed he knew everyone in the county.

Bayles remembered his father fondly, remarking, "They broke the mold when they made him."

It wasn't only in bars that Billee spent his free time. Between World Wars I and II, Nims Lake was the place to be for socializing in the area. A man-made lake developed from a low-lying rice field, it boasted a two-sided bathhouse, springboards, a two-level tower, and a dance pavilion. Despite his well-known reputation as a drinker, Billee never generated rumors of inappropriateness with other women. He just liked to have a good time socially and loved to dance, so Nims Lake was an important stop for him. Years later one of Bayles's law clients remarked on her memories of Billee at Nims Lake.

"Your daddy was the best dancer in Fort Mill," she told him.

Though he himself was not a drinker, Bayles's similar personality and social habits, dancing included, would spark rumors about his own life in later years. It was just one of the ways he learned from his father's example. An only child himself, Billee showed his only child how to relate to others—how to learn what was important to them and then figure out how he could help them achieve it. He was a born politician, serving on the city council and the school board and narrowly losing his race for mayor. More importantly, he was the local Democratic Executive Committeeman and ward heeler—a political operative who uses his influence on behalf of his party in a given electoral area. He used his talents behind the scenes, another important lesson he would pass on to his son. He would also have strong opinions about where Bayles should be educated, having purposely skipped any association with Davidson because his own father, William Sr., had been a star there. Instead, Billee chose Washington and Lee in Virginia for his undergraduate studies. When he finished there in 1925, he took a detour to radio school to learn to repair the instruments and opened a shop in New York but eventually made his way to Cumberland University Law School in Lebanon, Tennessee (now Samford University). By the time he and Libba were married in 1930, Billee had passed the bar and was ready to assume the mantle as Fort Mill's first lawyer.

Billee continued to frequent drinking establishments with his good friend John Spratt, who founded the Bank of Fort Mill. He and Spratt, both sons of privilege, could often be found hanging out together in bars with their drivers cooling their heels until the scions were ready to call it a night. Eventually Libba had had enough of the carousing and upon their arrival at the Mack home one evening, she instructed the drivers to take them to Billee's office rather than bring them into the house. It was the office Billee had built beside the Banks Street house in 1941 so his father could retire to Fort Mill and join him in the practice. William Sr. had died in New York later that same year before he could make the move. Now years later, Billie and Spratt, who had ventured quite deep into their cups that night, slept off the effects of alcohol in that law office surrounded by books published by Billee's father.

It was quite an ignominious end to an evening out.

*

Libba's concern for the impact of drink didn't end with Billee. Each weekend she would pick up children whose parents were known to be weekend imbibers. This included some of her own nieces and nephews. She would bring them to her house, and as a result, Bayles was able to get to know his Mills cousins well. Libba began to take on the role of matriarch for that side of the family as her mother, Ziza, grew older. Bayles grew quite close to some of his cousins, three in particular. Libba's brother John Barron (J. B.) Jr. had one child; a daughter named Betty. Bayles and Betty, who was two years older, loved to play baseball, and each was known to occasionally eschew a bit of time during the grammar school day to walk directly across the street for a visit with their grandmother. After J. B. Sr.'s death in 1929, Ziza let the upstairs rooms to teachers. She lived downstairs, with four female educators upstairs. Betty lived with her parents in a house her father built right next door to the one their grandfather had constructed. It was so easy to pop over to one of the houses that it made sense to the children to just walk on over if they thought they needed to.

In fact, one of Betty's sojourns to her own house to show her mother the tooth she had just lost resulted in a school-wide assembly the next day in which the principal, her uncle no less, made an announcement to the entire school: "I need to impress something on you people. You are not to leave the school ground without permission."

Betty recalled the story years later, saying, "I nearly died because everybody knew it was me!"

Bayles was more apt to slip away just because he could, and when he left it was generally for the remainder of the day. Sometimes he would actually walk from the parking lot at First Baptist Church, where his mother would drop him off in the morning, directly past the school next door and on to his grandmother's house. After school, sometimes he would venture up to Main Street and hang out at the drug store, but he would always make a point to be back at his grandmother's house by the time Libba was scheduled to pick him up after work. His skipping school didn't please Libba, who wanted him always to do the right thing. Even when he was rebellious, he knew his mother was deserving of respect, hence his showing up where he was supposed to be at least by pickup time.

Mother and son would occasionally argue, especially once he was in high school. Always a social animal, Bayles was frequently out with friends. Libba would ask about who he was going out with and would often caution him if she felt his friends were of questionable morals. Like most teenagers, he would insist he knew best and proceed with his plans, but he and his mother would always come around and make peace.

In an attempt to make sure her privileged son developed an understanding of how those without wealthy grandfathers as benefactors earned a living, she told him he needed to take a job in the cotton mill to get a taste of the real world. He spent three weeks working at the Fort Mill #1 plant during the summer after high school. He knew a friend who was going to be working there too, and he thought he would see him and they could pal around while on the job, but he quickly realized he wouldn't even see his friend because of the sheer size of the plant. The style-setting leader of his pack of friends got no special treatment in the mill. He started at the bottom as a sweeper.

"I learned a lot about mills, about weaving, doffing, that kind of stuff. But I was just the lowest person on the totem pole when I was working there. It was hard work, but it was not that bad. I was young so I didn't think it was that bad. But I can imagine for the other people working there that they had a much tougher job than I did. And the pay was—well, it was a textile mill. You couldn't pay much because you had to sell your product. But the Springs Mills were better than any of the other mills around because the Colonel took care of his folks."

His brief time doing shift work in the mill gave Bayles an appreciation for how hard people had to work to provide for their families. It was a lesson he never forgot, one of many he credits to his mother. He recalls her talking often about moral courage. Part of that involved encouraging him not to be afraid to speak out when he saw something wasn't right. It was an admonition he would come back to throughout his life. Whether he achieved the standard she tried to instill in him or not, when faced with moral questions he would remember her teachings and yearn for the ability to live up to them.

Toward the end of their lives, Libba and Billee depended on Bayles to take care of bills and see to their care after Billee had run through his large inheritance just as he promised he would.

Libba suffered with low blood pressure for years, and in 1984 Bayles got a call at his beach house in Ocean Drive, near Myrtle Beach, from her doctor, who had just come from seeing her on a house call. He told Bayles he wanted to send her to the hospital in Rock Hill for further tests. Bayles told the doctor he preferred that she be sent to a different hospital, in Charlotte, but the doctor assured him he didn't plan to keep her in the hospital and that it would be a quick in and out stop.

Before Bayles had left for the beach, he had stopped by his parents' house to see them as he did most days when he finished work at the law office that was next door. He and Libba had gotten into an argument and he left after they had heated words. He started for the beach and made it about half an hour down the road when his conscience got to him, so he turned around and went back to Fort Mill. He and Libba spent another hour talking and smoothed things over. He left a second time after peace had been restored. It was the last time he would see her outside of a hospital setting. The call from the doctor had come just two days after their argument.

Once Libba arrived at the hospital for her tests, her condition worsened and she was admitted to the ICU. She died a few days later, on September 15, of heart failure.

Billee continued to live in the house on Banks Street after Libba's death. A smoker most of his life, Billee had given up the habit at the age of seventy-eight, but the damage to his lungs had been done. Bayles cared for him as long as he was able, but it became apparent before long that Billee would need to go to a skilled-care facility. Once he was settled in to the center, his social nature asserted itself and he spent most of his time in a wheelchair mingling with nurses and other patients rather than in his room. Still, he wasn't happy about his surroundings and let Bayles know it whenever he stopped by for a visit.

"There's the son of a bitch who brought me here," he would tell the nurses.

Though he would brush it off afterward as though he had been kidding, it still stung and Bayles never forgot the feeling. Billee lived for six months after he moved to the care facility and passed away on March 15, 1986.

The deaths of his parents when Bayles was in his 50s had a tremendous impact on his own life, but he would spend his remaining years recalling their lessons and keeping their memories alive through stories and remembrances. Some of the times he liked to remember best were from his years as a young man growing up while they were in their prime and he was becoming his own person under their care.

YOUNG BAYLES
AND THE BOYS

Bayles always liked getting involved in things. But he was
careful not to be the perpetrator.

—Jimmy Howie, childhood friend

Fort Mill Grammar School, located right across the street from his grandmother's house on Confederate Street, was Bayles's first foray into formal education. When he started first grade, students went to grammar school for six grades and then on to high school in seventh, finishing there after grade eleven. By the time Bayles entered high school, twelfth grade had been added to the program. He would graduate with forty-two others in the Fort Mill High School class of 1952, the last class to graduate from the building situated on Tom Hall Street. During his school years, his penchant for being social meant he was always surrounded by a group of friends, and they got in to quite a variety of antics.

As the only child of a father with a reputation as a hellion in his time, Bayles was prone to adventures that would cause his mother no end of concern. In grammar school, the hijinks were quite tame, but he and friends Clifford Belt and Jimmy Dinkins did find themselves in hot water in fifth grade during lunch break from Ms. Mosley's class. The three boys made a habit of bringing their lunch to school in brown bags so they would have free time during the lunch period instead of having to walk anywhere to get something to eat. One day they decided to use this time to do some creative writing on the blackboard in a classroom located under the school auditorium. As with most groups of preadolescent boys of nearly any era, their thoughts tended toward anything to do with girls. What they wrote on the board was comprised mainly of lewd comments guaranteed to make ten-year-old boys snicker. Unfortunately, the noise they made drew the attention of the school's principal, Reighton Richards. Ms. Richards was the sister of a congressman, the niece of a governor, and one of Grandmother Ziza Mills' boarders, and she did not tolerate shenanigans. Caught in the act, chalk in hand, the three boys found themselves on a forced march to her office, where Ms. Richards promptly administered a liberal application of corporal punishment.

The three of them managed to find trouble outside of school as well. Clifford and Jimmy would sometimes visit Bayles at his grandmother's house across the street from the school, where there was an outhouse located in the back. They found it a convenient place to light up some "rabbit tobacco."

Classmate Jimmy Howie lived on Spring Street when he and Bayles began a friendship that would last a lifetime. He recalls a time in grammar school when teacher Lib Mills, Bayles's aunt, staged a mock trial event. Jimmy was the prosecutor and Bayles was assigned the role of defense attorney. The class decided Bayles had the better argument so the judgment went in his favor. In another case of foreshadowing, Bayles would devote his career in the law predominately to defense work, with the exception of work done as city attorney. Howie recalled Bayles having an interest in politics from an early age as a result of an uncle, Cody Smith, running for office. Howie remembered a young Bayles showing an interest in the campaign.

Bayles might also be found down at Luke Patterson's store at the corner of Banks and Tom Hall Streets, where he would meet up with Billy Barron. Billy and Judy Brown were the only kids Bayles knew from school who lived near him. They would ride their bikes all the way over to Doby's Bridge Road and pick up a friend, Gene Ward. At night the boys would play a game with the traffic making its way down Doby's Bridge, which was still a dirt road. They would stand on each side of the road holding a slack rope. They would pull it taut when they saw a car approaching. Drivers wouldn't see the rope until they were close enough for their headlights to reach it and then they would lock up the breaks and end up screeching to a halt sideways in the road.

But Bayles wasn't always getting into mischief. Since he enjoyed spending time at Rogers Drug Store on Main Street from a young age, it evolved naturally that he would help Elizabeth Rogers, the pharmacist's wife, make and deliver her famous sandwiches that would sell out quickly each Saturday morning. Merchant Joseph Brown of the Belk Brown department store had two sons, Joe and Bobby, with whom Bayles would spend hours playing war games in the woods.

One particular pastime consistently scored high marks with the group of friends. Bayles was experienced in traveling by train from the passenger depot at the foot of Main Street. The monthly trips his family took to visit his grandfather in New York gave him a certain worldly cachet among the other boys. Billee would load up a group of the boys and drop them off at the depot with a handful of coins. For a dime each, they could buy a ticket on the number 31 train and ride it the nine miles across the state line to nearby Pineville. For another dime they could buy a return ticket on the number 32 and ride it back to Fort Mill. It felt like a grand adventure in freedom for the youngsters.

The boys found their spare time for antics curtailed somewhat when they made it to Fort Mill High in seventh grade and started playing organized team sports. Bayles played baseball and basketball for Coach Marshall Edwards, though his reputation in basketball wasn't as a star player. As a junior varsity player, he got to watch and learn from his cousin Buddy Mills and teammates Johnny Neal, Boozy Munn, and Ray Sparks. By his junior year he had made the varsity team with fellow players David Ward, Leonard "Chubby" Strauss, Rabbit Brown, and Dick Covington. An "A" school based on size, Fort Mill regularly played against area teams York, Clover, Great Falls, and Kershaw. At the game where he was to make his reputation in the sport, he was playing in the guard position against Great Falls. His teammate, (and Fort Mill's star football player), Dick Covington, 210 pounds and over six feet tall, was also a star on the basketball court and played center. The game rules in those days called for a jump ball to determine possession much more frequently than modern rules. When this happened, Covington's height gave him the advantage and he would often tip the ball to Bayles, who would attempt to take it to the basket and score. It was common for rural schools in that era to have their auditoriums do double-duty as gymnasiums, and games were regularly held on the stages of these halls, making chasing out-of-bounds balls especially entertaining.

At this game on the stage at Great Falls Auditorium, Bayles had scored the opening points of the game on a tip from Covington. By halftime he was the game's leading scorer, but not just for Fort Mill. Upon having the boy he was guarding suddenly move to a new floor position followed by an unexpected loose ball, Bayles had eagerly retrieved the ball and sent it to the basket, scoring again—only this time for the opposing team. When his man had moved, Bayles had gotten confused as to where they were on the court. He ended up doing that twice and went to the half having scored eight points—four for each team. Coach Edwards pulled him aside and pointed across the floor at Speedy Starnes, the coach for Great Falls.

"You see that fellow over there?" the coach asked. "He wants you to be on his team—and if you do that again, you *will* be."

Baseball was a bit better fit for Bayles, mostly as a result of his commitment to it. Playing again under the direction of Coach Edwards, he got a more encouraging word this time.

Edwards told him, "You're one of the best players I've got. You have no natural ability, but you work at it."

Coach Edwards didn't pull any punches when communicating with his players. Still, he may have taken some extra care with Bayles, because it was Bayles's father who had saved his coaching job not long before. The coach played pro football in the Dixie League for the Charlotte Clippers, and they held games on Sunday. Fort Mill's mayor at the time, Frank Lytle, felt the coach was setting a bad example for students by engaging in games on the Lord's day. He approached the school board with a request to have the coach fired. The board at the time was chaired by the honorable William Mack—Billee. Several of Coach Edwards' football players showed up at the Mack house to lobby on the coach's behalf.

"Frank Lytle does not run the school," he assured the players. "He's the mayor of the town. I promise you Coach Edwards won't be fired."

Chairman Mack was true to his word and the coach kept his job. The elder Mack had little use for purely pious protestations.

*

Even before high school, Bayles had entered the work world. At the age of twelve he had taken on his first paying job working for William Bradford, the publisher of *The Fort Mill Times.* His job was to fold the freshly printed newspapers, put on the delivery labels, and haul them by the bagful to the post office. That same year he remembers when his uncle's hardware store on Main Street caught fire and he helped carry out the inventory they could salvage and drop it at his grandmother's house, two blocks away. Uncle J. B. immediately got the business up and going again and Bayles would sometimes work for him during summer vacation while he was in college. Within two years of starting his newspaper job, he gained even more freedom when he got his driver's license. A license could be obtained at age fourteen in those days, and Bayles had plenty of reason to want one—the Mack family owned two Studebakers. Having a license meant he could drive his friends around when his parents would let him use one of the cars, and it also meant he could earn income driving local doctor J. B. Elliott on his house call rounds in the doctor's new Chrysler. Once Bayles had wheels, that essentially meant all his friends had wheels, and the level and frequency of the antics began to ratchet up.

Childhood friend Jimmy Howie remembers many youthful pranks in the company of Bayles, including one run through town with Bayles clocking in at 126 miles per hour. Jimmy was also on board along with Jerry Griffin when the boys decided to put a cherry bomb in Miss Nora Harris's mailbox. They thought it would make a loud noise, but they didn't expect the resulting explosion that blew the mailbox apart. It was a moment eerily similar to his father's shattering of the windows at a friend's house in his youth. The boys found out soon after the incident that damaging mailboxes was a federal offense, so they took to tossing the cherry bombs at the brick walls of houses instead. One night five of the boys went driving through Whiteville Park, which was sometimes referred to as "Mortgage Hollow" because of the nice houses being built there. They tossed their cherry bombs out the car windows as they drove. One of the incendiary balls hit a pole and bounced back into the car, fuse lit and burning down quickly. All of them jumped out of the car, Bayles the driver included. The car kept rolling slowly and the bomb went off, after which the boys got back in and continued doing the exact same thing. Young people can be slow to learn their lessons.

Despite Bayles's good grades, above 90 percent in all his classes, he managed to get himself kicked out of the Beta Club in high school because of his abysmal grade in deportment. His score was so low that it brought his overall average down enough to make him academically ineligible for club membership. The poor grade can be best understood by looking at some of the incidents that resulted in disciplinary actions. Next door to the high school was a fruit and vegetable cannery. During the school day some of the space was used as the high school cafeteria, where students could pick up lunch. One day Bayles and some friends picked up a big basket of oranges and decided to make a game of seeing if they could hurl them through a small opening at the top of the windows of the school's chemistry lab.

They managed to get a few inside before the principal, Jasper Taylor, caught them. He gave them their choice of a whipping or suspension. Bayles chose suspension, but Principal Taylor knew the boy's father was chairman of the school board and decreed he would have a whipping instead.

On another occasion, the basketball team and band had traveled to an away game, and the bus with the ballplayers had made it back to school before the band bus. Knowing band director Ben Stevenson was on the bus with the band, Bayles and his teammates took the opportunity to take the wheels off his car and set it up on Coca Cola crates. They managed to get themselves yet another whipping.

Study hall was located next door to the library. Bayles and Jimmy Howie would sneak over and lie on the library tables and go to sleep. Librarian Myrtle Wallace would ignore then and go about her business, but when the study hall teacher realized they had slipped out, she would show up in the library yielding a yardstick and chase them back where they belonged. The boys were regular connoisseurs of classic mid-twentieth-century high school shenanigans.

There was a ray of hope that they might clean up their acts as local police chief Raleigh Phillips took an interest in taking the boys on fishing excursions on the Catawba River at Sugar Creek or Lake Wylie. On one trip they were scheduled to spend the night at Joe Griffin's father's cabin on the lake. Phillips went to work setting up the fire for cooking the fish while the boys walked down to the water's edge, baited their hooks, and waited for a bite. At least that's what Phillips thought they were doing. What he may not have realized was the method they were using to pull quite an impressive haul of fish out of the water. Bayles's father had some old military crank-style telephones that the boys had commandeered to ensure their fishing expedition would be a success. They put the metal ends in the water and cranked the phones. The electricity generated sent the catfish to the surface where the boys basically scooped them up. They collected hundreds of pounds of fish. On another occasion they took out Mr. Griffin's motorboat with a pig onboard, causing a commotion among the onlookers on the banks.

The Studebaker was also handy for transporting stolen watermelons as the boys found out one night when Bayles parked the car down the road from Sam Smith's watermelon field. He waited there while the other boys brought out forty of the melons and loaded them in the car, filling the trunk first and then the back seat. They went to the bandstand and ate some of their pilfered loot there, then took the rest to Culp Brothers ice plant. A friendly employee there put the melons in the back of the plant to keep them fresh and cold. The boys would go by night after night and he would have left two or three out for them until they were all gone.

Regi Thackston had moved to Fort Mill in seventh grade and quickly become part of the group, taking part in the cherry bombing and the fruit stealing. It was Regi who had a talent for locating watermelon fields and peach orchards where the boys could count on a good haul and little chance of detection. But fruit pilfering wasn't the boys' only pastime. Regi remembers Bayles always had money to order plenty of fireworks. One night they took a supply of skyrockets to the high school football field to shoot them off, but the bottles tipped over after the fuses were lit, sending the incendiary payloads in the direction of the boys themselves. The pranksters also wrought havoc with the local police by pulling levers at electrical power switchboxes that plunged entire neighborhoods into darkness until someone could reset the switch.

At school, they pranked their teacher by pretending Jimmy Howie suffered from seizures. He would surreptitiously gather bits of chalk from the classroom and then chew on them while dramatically writhing on the floor. Their teacher, Ms. O'Neal, was horrified.

Sometimes they could be found at Rexall Pool Hall, where the pool tables and the urinals shared the same large room. Patrons could "shoot, spit, and pee" all in one place. In his senior yearbook in the popular senior will and testament section, Bayles proudly predicted he would one day be the owner of the Rexall Pool Hall. As it turned out, it wasn't an empty boast.

Most of the boys' time was spent in less destructive or terrifying pursuits. Whether meant as a derogatory term or not, the boys embraced their reputation in town as "drugstore cowboys," considering it a badge of coolness and adding to their adolescent swagger. They idled over burgers and milkshakes at local soda shop counters where the popular kids congregated. Most days after school they would make their way to a parking meter just outside Martin's Drug Store on Main Street, where they would hang out talking to girls until the old men who normally occupied the town's bandstand next door headed home in the late afternoon. Then the boys would take over the bandstand, where according to Regi, they would "tell jokes and lies!"

But more often than not they could be found in Bayles's car driving around town listening to music. They would also take in movies at the old Majestic, which was located on the very spot on Confederate Street where Bayles's railcar office sits today. In high school it was replaced by the Center Theater at the foot of Main Street and the boys followed. Regi Thackston fondly remembers time spent "dragging Main," going up and down the street in Bayles's car to see and be seen. Sometimes they would retire to the Mack house or its adjacent law office to listen to Bayles's large collection of records that he would order from the legendary Randy's Record Mart in Gallatin, Tennessee. He would even bring his collection to the teen "canteen" dances held at the golf and country club on Saturday nights.

"The music was always the best around Bayles, because he ordered the best," recalled Regi more than sixty-five years later.

During the high school years and in the summers after graduation, Bayles and his group of friends did have occasion to bear witness to incidents much more serious than some tossed cherry bombs or watermelon heists. Fort Mill and Rock Hill are towns separated by the Catawba River. In the earliest days when the country was still young, the only way across the river was to ford it. The best place to get across came to be known as the Nation Ford, in reference to the Catawba Indians who were the area's first inhabitants. By Bayles's day there was a bridge across the water on Highway 21 and youth from both banks had a habit of posturing in an effort to discourage groups of teens from one side from venturing over to the opposite side.

"We kind of prided ourselves on watching for people. If somebody from Rock Hill came over here, we'd sort of say, 'Hey, how 'bout y'all go on?'" Bayles recalled the "taunting" with a laugh.

It was all teenage bravado, but the drugstore cowboys imagined they were looking out for the town's best interests with their vigilance. There were exceptions to the rules of the river crossings, however. Just over on the Rock Hill side of the bridge, a grouping of dive bars and restaurants had cropped up and the boys just out of high school would head over there to places like Porter's. They would watch people getting thrown out for fighting, mostly soldiers down from Fort Bragg and mill workers. One evening the boys were hanging out while a pretty waitress, Thelma "Boots" Slagle, rumored to be the daughter of an alleged bootlegger, worked her shift. One of the young boys had a crush on her so the group would spend time at Porter's so he could see her. She was a married woman who nonetheless was engaged to another man and reportedly dating yet another, a Rock Hill businessman. Within a couple of weeks, the dismembered body of Rock Hill businessman George C. Beam Jr. was found stuffed in a wooden crate in nearby Crowder's Creek. Nathan "Nat" Corn was charged with the murder. Corn was the fiancé of Boots Slagle and she would testify on his behalf at the trial. The local paper fawned over her physical appearance in court.

"The defendant's fiancé, trimly attired in a green suit, a rose-colored blouse open at the throat, and with her hair in an upswept braid, testified that she had been with Corn all Saturday night and practically all day Sunday," read the local coverage.[27]

It was high drama.

Corn was found guilty and given the death penalty. He was scheduled to die just six weeks after the verdict. Justice tended to move swiftly in those days. The scheduled execution date, January 28, 1949, was a mere seven months after the murder itself. After the trial, Bayles's young friend actually went on a few dates with the newly single Slagle, but when word got out that Corn had escaped from prison, the friend, seven years younger than his paramour, skipped town to hide out while the convicted murderer was on the lam. Corn was caught three weeks later in Springfield, Illinois, but then staged a second escape that earned him freedom for six months before he was recaptured in Los Angeles. Once Bayles's friend had returned from hiding, he didn't take up with Slagle again. He wisely opted to stay away from what surely was a dangerous situation. He later married and settled down happily in Fort Mill.

Most of their forays into Rock Hill didn't include hanging out in the vicinity of murderers, but they were often prime occasions for stirring up a little fast-car action. Another of their haunts near the river was the Bob-In, where the waitresses brought the food right to the cars. Sometimes they would meet up with some Rock Hill boys who wanted to test both the speed of their cars and the strength of their wits against the boys from Fort Mill. A race would ensue from the Bob-In, travel across the river and up highway 21 past the Peach Stand, and head on to Brandon's Grill near the North Carolina line.

Other nights in Rock Hill the boys would venture farther into the city and go dancing at Darlene's on India Hook, where there was a concrete dance floor.

But not all was antics and mischief with Bayles and his band of brothers. To a man, Bayles was more well-off than his friends and lived a lifestyle that was different from theirs. To some it was completely foreign.

When Regi Thackston's family arrived in Fort Mill during the boys' seventh-grade year, they moved in with his grandmother in a house on Ardrey Street beside the mill. The house had no indoor plumbing and the family was quite poor. There was no expectation for Regi that he could expect a future much different than the life he knew. Meeting Bayles introduced Regi to the possibility of something more. Regi had chosen the "college track" for his curriculum at Fort Mill High, although he had no idea how he would be able to afford to go. Bayles "adopted" Regi and made sure he had transportation to go places and clothing that helped him fit in with his peers, taking away some of the stigma that can be so hard on teenagers.

Bayles was the unofficial leader of his group of friends, but it seemed to have come about naturally. He was elected class president each year of high school except his senior year, and teenagers flocked to him in much the same way adults were drawn to his father. He had a natural sense of style and the funds to carry it off, so he became the fashion style-setter among his friends, encouraging them to dress as successful up-and-coming young men and filling in the gaps when the other boys couldn't afford to emulate his sartorial finery. The boys did their best to emulate Bayles's style with Regi even learning to tailor his own pants on a sewing machine.

Tailored pants were important in early 1950s wear; pegged trousers with pocket flaps were de rigueur. There were cuffs and welt seams, and the pegging should be tight enough that you had to take off your socks to put on your pants. Flashy pistol flaps were in style, and for denim it had to be Levi's, bought with advance thought as to the length needed for the desired roll-up.

"If you wore a thirty-inch inseam you bought a thirty-nine so you could do one single long roll-up," Regi explained.

Bayles also recommended cashmere sweaters (from Nathan's in Rock Hill), which were worn without an undershirt if one really wanted to look cool. Pants were worn low on the hips (*low* being a relative term given more modern and questionable trends in low-slung jeans) and never with a belt.

Jimmy Howie also remembered shopping with Bayles for denim jackets at Ezra Munn's Men's Store. Eventually Bayles had them all wearing blue suede shoes. They topped off their ensembles with ducktail haircuts. The boys from Fort Mill may not have all been rich dandies, but they looked the part.

It could have been a tricky predicament, but all the boys agree that Bayles didn't lord his financial advantages over them. In fact, they recall just the opposite. They remember a friend who went out of his way to share what he had with them. Regi Thackston was the beneficiary of clothing that Bayles no longer wore.

"Half of my clothes at college were things he had outgrown," he recalled.

And Bayles wasn't generous just with unneeded clothing or a few dollars at the movie theater or the drugstore soda fountain. Every summer from the time Bayles was eight years old, his family would spend time at the beach in one of the towns near North Myrtle. Billee bought a house in Windy Hill and later sold it and rented a house in Ocean Drive for their annual six-week sojourn. The area is the birthplace of the famous shag dance and is still ground zero for aficionados who come every summer to dance in the pavilions at the water's edge. It was paradise for teen boys and Bayles started inviting friends to join him once he was old enough to come and go around the beach town without his parents. Jimmy Howie was a frequent guest summer after summer.

In the late 1940s and early 50s there was little mixing of the races in social settings and the boys remember making their way back to the Ocean Drive house at night once the dancing was finished and having to walk through Atlantic Beach, which was primarily an African-American enclave. The boys would stay away from the shore to avoid trouble, walking waist deep in the water through that section.

When the Macks decamped to the beach for the summer they would bring along their cook to keep them in meals while the socializing was in full swing. Occasionally, likely for want of material in the sleepy summertime, the local newspaper, *The Fort Mill Times*, would send a reporter to visit the Macks at the beach and then report on the happenings in the paper's social column. When it came out,

Billee would read it to the boys, embellishing it for effect, and have them roaring with laughter at what the folks back home must think of their adventures.

Regi Thackston was invited to the beach house when the boys were in high school and he called it a seminal moment in his life.

"I was sixteen or seventeen when I saw the ocean for the first time. We were in the back seat of Bayles's dad's car," he recalls, when they crested a hill and he could see the vast ocean in front of him.

At night they would make their way to the pavilion, but Regi didn't know how to dance. He noticed the girls seemed to pay the most attention to the good dancers so he set about learning to shag.

Bayles's cousin Gilbert "Buddy" Mills was two years older and considered a big man on campus to the younger boys. He would come to the beach to spend part of the summer with them and teach them things about being grown up. Jimmy Howie recalled Buddy teaching him "to walk properly on my heels and not bob up and down." It was Buddy who also counseled the boys when it was time to leave behind their high school ways and start acting like men. He lectured them on how to dress and how to have better relationships with girls.

"We hung on his every word," Howie remembered.

After high school Bayles and friends would still head to the coast in the off-season, often without having arranged for a place to stay. They would get into town and find a place to crash for the night, grab a bite to eat, and head to the pavilion, where there were always pretty girls ready to dance.

A love for shag dancing and the beach has stayed with Bayles throughout his life. As an adult he built a house for his family in Ocean Drive, completing construction in 1974. Even into his eighties, each September for his birthday he hosts some of those same friends from childhood to relive the glorious summer nights of their youth.

The boys who could be found hanging out in front of Martin's Drug Store during high school had good reason to listen to cousin Buddy and the other boys who had an extra two or three years of maturity—they were all girl crazy. It was an era still hanging on to 1930s and 40s standards of acceptable conduct for courting. The free-wheeling mores of the 60s were still a few years in the future, and high school boys had to deal with more than just overprotective fathers. They had to manage even tougher gatekeepers looking out for the girls they wanted to date—their mothers. It was still a June Cleaver world, and even if the fictional June did seem oblivious to Eddie Haskell's obsequious overtures, she would likely have been a lot less willing to buy his act if Wally and the Beav had had a sister in the house. Mothers in the late 40s and early 50s, especially Southern ones, were on high alert for anything that might threaten their daughters' reputations. That meant a boy who might be perfectly acceptable for an afternoon milkshake at the drugstore counter need not expect that to translate to a standing invitation to come by the house at 6:30 for a date.

Going out in pairs seemed to appease the sensibilities of overprotective parents to a degree, and the Fort Mill drugstore cowboys learned to use that loophole to their advantage. Sometimes that meant two boys got to go out with two girls they liked. Often it meant one of the boys and one of the girls would end up playing the roles of wingman and wingwoman—reluctant "chaperones" rather than excited double-daters.

Regi Thackston found himself making up half of the other couple many times. He remembered when Bayles's mother wanted to make sure her son was associating with "quality girls" and Betty Lockman topped the list. She was from a good family and was a popular girl in school. But Betty had a cousin visiting and she couldn't go out and leave the girl at home. So Regi was called into action to be the date for Betty's cousin. "Date" may have been an overstatement. Regi recalled the evening mostly consisted of them all sitting in the Lockman's living room talking and laughing. Bayles and Betty went out for a while, and if Regi wasn't available, Jimmy Howie could usually be counted on to take his place. All the boys were enjoying spending time with the girls they liked, or at least finding ways to make sure their paths would cross. Bayles could be found squiring different girls around town including Marie Shaw, Peggy Oliver, and a second Betty, this time Betty Ann McKibben.

Regi recalled how a Friday night might go. "Girls socially had very little freedom away from home," he said. They generally had early curfews by 10 p.m. After the boys saw their dates home, they would meet up at the bandstand and wait for the late movie at the Center Theater across the street to let out. There were a couple of girls who worked at the theater in concessions.

"We'd wait at the bandstand and walk or drive the girls home," Regi remembered.

They were reveling in their freedom and youth and testing the boundaries of what their girlfriends, who had been dutifully delivered home for their early curfews, would tolerate.

But all that ended their junior year when Jimmy Howie wanted Bayles to play wingman to him. Jimmy's girlfriend was in a lower grade as the high school at that time included everything from seventh grade to twelfth. He told Bayles he too should consider dating younger girls.

Bayles, in typical upperclassman form, asked, "Who is worth dating in eighth, ninth, or tenth grade?" Pretty soon he found out.

Students would leave the school grounds for lunch that was set up at the cannery across the street from the town's armory. Bayles and Jimmy Howie were in Ms. Lytle's home economics class one day when Bayles looked out the window and noticed a group of girls sitting under a tree behind the school eating their lunches. One young lady in particular got his attention. He asked Jimmy who the pretty dark-haired girl was, but Jimmy didn't know. Undeterred, Bayles hopped out of the window and walked over to where they were sitting. He looked at the dark-haired girl and asked where she was going after school. She said she planned to go to Martin's Drug Store. He asked if he could go with her and she told him that would be all right. Bayles headed back inside the school to rejoin his class. Ms. Lytle was surprised to see him walk in the classroom door. She hadn't noticed him leaving through the window earlier.

After school Bayles carried the girl's books on their walk over to Martin's. They sat down in a booth and Bayles made his move.

"I was thinking this Friday you ought to go out with me," he blurted out.

She told him she would have to ask her parents and let him know and he went on to baseball practice. The next day she found him and told him her parents had agreed to let her go out with him. They went out that weekend. Her father was strict, but soon she asked Bayles to the Sadie Hawkins dance to be held at the old armory on Main Street. He said yes. They were high school sweethearts after that.

They would break up in college, get back together, and eventually walk down the aisle. But that was all still to come the day he hopped out of the window of Ms. Lytle's classroom to talk to her for the first time.

Her name was Joanne Arnold and she was in the ninth grade. Bayles got the answer to the question he had asked Jimmy about who was worth dating in the lower grades. Joanne Arnold was—and that was that.

*

The boys Bayles spent his formative years with, now all in their 80s, influenced each other's lives in ways that resonate still today.
"Everyone always looked up to the Macks and the Mills [families]," Howie recalled. He especially remembered the great respect he had for Elizabeth Mack and how kind she was to him.

Regi Thackston goes even further: "I owe a lot to Bayles. He was my best friend growing up, and I have a great appreciation for how he brought me out of the mill hill. He introduced me to another way of life."

Regi Thackston would go on to graduate from Wofford College and then head to Emory University to earn his master of theology degree. He became a respected pastor. The shy boy who learned to sew to tailor his own clothes and often wore hand-me-downs, the same boy who once watched from the sidelines, would go on to serve on Wofford's Board of Trustees alongside Anne Springs Close, the daughter of the owner of the mills and the town's wealthiest man. As a teenager he could not have imagined moving in the same circles. His beloved Wofford later honored him with an honorary doctorate of divinity degree, so he's Dr. Regi Thackston now—a long way from the mill hill.

The boys were on the cusp on manhood, each with his own path to take. Bayles would choose his next move with a nod toward the path his grandfather William had taken many years prior. William had made a success of himself and lent honor and prestige to the Mack name. As all good Southern gentlemen are raised to understand, Bayles knew looking back could be the best roadmap for going forward.

WASHINGTON, LEE, AND TWENTIETH-CENTURY WAR

Lex dabit remedium
The law will give a remedy.

—from the Latin

Harriet Hudson Banks Mack spent countless hours with her great grandson Bayles on the porch with the tree growing up through it. Though she passed away when he was not yet four years old, she left him a legacy from her own lineage, one that would continue to factor in successive generations: a commitment to education. Harriet's only sibling was a younger brother, Alexander Robinson Banks, known to all as A. R. Born in Chester County when Harriet was two, A. R. would make a mark on the education community in Fort Mill before organized public schools were the norm. Their father, William, was a first-generation American, his father having emigrated from Scotland in 1793. William was an ordained minister, like the man Harriet would eventually marry, J. B. Mack. The Civil War intruded on A. R.'s young life, and by its waning days he was old enough to give brief service to the Confederacy. After that, his life was his own and he headed across the state line to North Carolina and to Davidson College, a step in the long line of ties the family has with the institution.

But theology was not his chosen path. A. R. graduated from Davidson in 1869 and embarked on a career as an educator that would stretch more than fifty years. The very first school in Fort Mill was a private preparatory school located on what would later be fittingly called Academy Street. Fort Mill Academy welcomed male students, charging tuition of $20 for a twenty-week session that included Latin and Greek. For an extra $9 per month, students could board. In 1875 A. R. Banks became the school's headmaster and was known about town as "Professor Banks." The school saw a great number of its students go on to higher education, particularly at Davidson College or the University of South Carolina. Accusations of favoritism toward these two universities followed A. R. after he left Fort Mill Academy in 1888 and continued his work at various other schools in South Carolina, but nobody could argue with his results. His students went on to successful careers in the law and in ministry after matriculation at a variety of top colleges, including Princeton.

Aside from the street where the academy stood being named in its honor, the street where Billee and Libba Mack were raising their son, Bayles, bore a reference to this ancestor as well. Previously called

Rocky Road, when Billee Mack built his new house and law office it had a new name: Banks Street.

By the time Bayles and his classmates graduated from Fort Mill High School in 1952, the link to Davidson College was firmly established in the Mack family. There was little question where he would earn his undergraduate degree. He enjoyed his time there, graduating in 1956 with a bachelor's degree in political science. The real question was where to go next. He knew he wanted a career in law, and where he should study was a topic his father felt strongly about. Billee wanted Bayles to choose Harvard or Yale. His good friend John Spratt Sr. was a Yale graduate, and Billee wanted the Ivy League for his own son. Bayles wasn't interested in either school. While he was doing his undergraduate work he had heard the way people talked about the new lawyers coming out of those venerated institutions.

"I found out at Davidson that if you go to Harvard or Yale and you come back to practice law in a country area or Charlotte, North Carolina, they didn't think much of you. But if you went to University of North Carolina or University of South Carolina or somewhere like that, everybody thought you were fine."

Bayles had his own list of criteria guiding his choice. He didn't want a "church school." Davidson College is affiliated with the Presbyterian Church (U.S.A.) and he felt he had already done that. He also didn't want a state-affiliated school once he heard of the experience of some students who were studying at the University of South Carolina. Today the Carolina law school is well-respected, but at that time they limited their curriculum to primarily South Carolina law, eschewing a broader legal education.

Billee hired a consultant to do a study of law schools, ranking the top Southern schools for consideration. His own undergraduate alma mater, Washington and Lee University in Lexington, Virginia, topped the list, followed by Vanderbilt and then Tulane. Further examination revealed Washington and Lee had more national recognition than the others and graduates of the program were handily recruited by impressive firms in New York and Washington, D.C. Long considered a "rich boys'" school, Washington and Lee was the Southern equivalent of the elite Brahmin institutions of the Northeast.

It was decided—to Virginia Bayles would go.

But times were not as simple as they had been when he had set off for Davidson four years earlier. Now the country was embroiled in a foreign war and young men were being sent to Korea to fight the Communists. Bayles had completed his ROTC training while at Davidson and upon graduation was commissioned into the army. At that time many people believed the war in Korea was drawing to a close. Bayles's great-uncle Murray Mack was the military mayor of Seoul and he called Bayles to report on the situation there.

He told his nephew, "There's no use in you coming over here. This is a police action now. We're through."

Bayles dutifully joined the Army Infantry Reserve unit in Rock Hill and had orders to report to Fort Sill for field artillery training the following February. During the summer between his Davidson graduation and beginning classes at Washington and Lee, Bayles drilled with his reserve unit, clerked in the York office of his father's friend John Spratt Sr., and worked for his uncle J. B. Mills in his hardware store in Fort Mill. It was a busy time and he was ready to settle down to his books when the term began. It wouldn't last long.

Just one semester into his studies, he received new military orders. Instead of field artillery at Fort Sill, he would be heading to Fort Bliss for training as a missile officer. The new assignment meant he would not be deployed to Korea, as all missile officers were stationed in Alaska, Greenland, and the US mainland and charged with domestic border protection.

With the specter of the Korean battlefield looming smaller in the distance, the time had come to see to his personal life. Before classes began at Washington and Lee, Bayles and Joanne Arnold had gotten engaged and they married on February 9, 1957. Shortly after the wedding, they reported to Fort Bliss in El Paso, Texas. They were expecting to move into housing on the post, but when they arrived, overcrowding meant there was nothing available. Instead, they were sent into town right on the Mexican border at Juárez crossing. They needed a place to live, and Bayles was about to make his first shrewd real estate deal.

An acquaintance told the young couple to head out Montana Road toward New Mexico and they would find some new construction there. Bayles and Joanne followed the directions and came upon a brand-new, U-shaped building containing about fifteen apartment units, all evidently empty. Across the street was rolling desert. A man was working in the yard area of the complex adding some landscaping, and they learned he was the landlord.

Uncle Sam was paying second lieutenants $252 a month in those days and Bayles saw a way to make the dollars stretch further. He proposed a deal with the landlord that would make Joanne the manager of the property. She would handle getting leases signed and the units rented, and in return the landlord would allow the Macks to rent on a month-to-month basis, since Bayles knew they would only be in the area for six months. The landlord, sensing he could get the young couple to take a substantial load off his plate, went one better. He told them if they would take over property management entirely, they could live there rent-free. It was a good deal for both sides, and the newlyweds had their first home together. They moved into the middle unit and started renting the others to fellow officers.

Bayles began his three-month classroom training in electronics and other specialty subjects. During that time he played in a fast-pitch softball league on the post, and when he finished the school portion of his training, he began to travel back and forth to White Sands, New Mexico, for additional training. White Sands was to be his permanent posting.

As part of his own officer training, he took over as battery commander in a battalion that had charge of $10 million in weapons. Responsibility for the inventory was signed it over to him. He was a twenty-two-year-old second lieutenant who had been in the service all of four months and suddenly found himself in the position of having to answer for a weapons pool that included 90-mm canons and 50-caliber machine guns among other types of guns, as well as the battery's allotment of ammunition. He realized when he started comparing the inventory list to what he could see with his own eyes that there was a discrepancy. These were large weapons, some measuring thirty to fifty feet in length. They were there as protection for the missile sites themselves. Luckily he had a capable, experienced sergeant under his command who knew how things really worked on site.

"It seems like there's a lot of midnight requisitioning going on here," he told the sergeant.

"There ain't no question," the sergeant responded.

The reality was that certain guns and even parts of guns like the long barrels were being taken apart and moved from battery to battery within the battalion according to the inspection schedule. That way, when a particular battery unit's turn rolled around, they would have a full complement of assigned weapons that matched the inventory list, thanks to the efforts of the non-commissioned officers. After that unit had passed inspection, the guns were moved to the next battery and so on, resulting in a continuous swap.

Bayles asked his sergeant if the missing weapons could be found. "We don't need to find them," the sergeant responded. "We can move them around." He wrapped up with some reassuring words for his commander. "I've got you covered, Lieutenant."

And so he did. It was a reality Bayles had heard about during basic training at Fort Benning between his junior and senior year at Davidson, but now he knew it was more than just a tale soldiers liked to tell. Years later he reflected on it.

"That was a rude awakening for me . . . a learning process. I had been warned that that happened all over the army. I'm sure it happened all over the military, but we just didn't have planes. In *theory*, they weren't gone off the base—but some had to be."

While he was still technically in training himself for his role, he was also responsible for training new recruits who would man the weapons. There was quite a bit of downtime because the units were not moved through training on a regular schedule. Sometimes they would have 200–250 troops on site and other times they would have none. Bayles spent part of that downtime with his commanding officer, a captain named Paul Manna, who bore an uncanny resemblance to decorated World War II veteran Audie Murphy. Manna was in charge of two other second lieutenants besides Bayles and they would often get together to shoot pool in the dayroom on post. Bayles would refer to him as "Captain Murphy."

When new troops did arrive, the officers would "troop the line" to meet and inspect them. One day when Bayles was making his way down a line of fresh troops, he saw a familiar face.

"Where you from soldier?"

"Fort Mill, South Carolina sir," came the reply.

"What's your name?"

The soldier responded with the last name of Howard.

"Are you 'Doodlebug' Howard?" Bayles asked.

"Yes, sir!"

In a desert on the other side of the country, young Mr. Howard had happened upon an officer from his hometown. They sat down later to talk about what was happening back in Fort Mill, no doubt a pleasant diversion for both men.

Desert-based training for the recruits included one very important lesson: don't touch the metal. Though White Sands had the benefit of cool, wet sand two feet under the surface, that bit of coolness didn't factor much during the daytime, when the temperature could get to 129 degrees. Big guns, plus the heat of firing, plus the heat of the unrelenting sun equaled hot metal, and one touch could do damage instantly. Lieutenant Mack did his best to warn them.

"I trained guys—'Don't touch the metal. Put your gloves on before you touch the metal because you're going to get fried and the only thing I can do about that is take you to the hospital. If you want to stay around this site and be with us, don't touch the metal.'"

Most heeded the warning, some forgot and paid the price, and some saw a way out of the sun for a while, albeit a painful one. After all, there was a military draft in place so plenty of men were there who would rather not be. Touching the metal was one way to get at least a brief respite from the New Mexico sun.

Back at Fort Bliss, Bayles was tapped for another task that leaned closer to his life outside the military. Owing to the single semester of law school he had completed, he was assigned to stand in defense of soldiers who found themselves on the wrong side of the Uniform Code of Military Justice. With the close proximity of the base to Juárez crossing, it was common for soldiers to break curfew and then try sneaking back across the border. There were holes in the fence at the Rio Grande, and the soldiers would come through those, often in an inebriated state and, worse yet, in uniform. Bayles was assigned to the Provost Marshall's office and part of his job was to accompany the personnel who patrolled the border, bringing in soldiers who violated the rules. The patrol would back up a van right at the fence and wait.

"We'd fill up the paddy wagon with eighteen or twenty of them."

The offenders were bound for the post jail, but sometimes Bayles or one of the other officers would give them a break.

"Sometimes we would take them to the post and give them two minutes to get back to the barracks, calling out, 'This is your lucky day!' I'd see them take off running. I never would put them in jail."

Still many did end up in the post jail, which meant they would have to face a "mini court martial" for what amounted to a misdemeanor. That's where Bayles came in. The men were typically very nervous, afraid of what would happen to them. He would assist by helping them present their own cases, which really amounted to them telling their stories to the court. Commanding officers served as judges to hear the cases, although they were prohibited from adjudicating any case of a soldier from their own unit. The defendant would stand to testify and Bayles would lead him through his story by asking some questions. It generally went something like this:

Bayles: *So you went into Mexico last night?*

Soldier: *Yes sir.*

Bayles: *Were you drinking?*

Soldier: *Yes, sir.*

Bayles: *Did you get with a woman?*

Soldier: *Yes, sir.*

Bayles: *And this woman kept you too long and you were unable to return to your post on time as you had planned to do?*

Solider [dim hope beginning to dawn on him]: *Yes, sir! That's what happened. I was there and planning to leave and be back by curfew and she just wouldn't let me leave, and when I finally did get out there was a big crowd at the crossing, and I just couldn't get through in time. But I surely did intend to, and I tried real hard!"*

Sometimes the punishment would be thirty days in the post jail or being made to "walk the guard" from 10 p.m. until 6 a.m. for ten days. But occasionally a soldier would get a lucky break and be let off with just a stern warning against breaking curfew again and a terse admonishment not to wear his uniform across the border. It's not impossible to imagine that the better the soldier was at feigning his earnest distress at not being able to get away from whatever woman factored into the story, the better his chances were of benefiting from any entertainment value his predicament may have offered the presiding commander.

Bayles and Joanne would sometimes cross the border themselves to spend some off time or to shop. Leather goods, particularly western boots, and copper items were cheap there, and they enjoyed furnishing their nest with their finds. Occasionally Bayles would go over with friends from the post and recalled there were always people selling things on the street. Children would tempt the soldiers with chewing gum, and if the soldiers didn't buy any, they would demonstrate a few extra words of English they had learned.

"American son of a bitch" was the standard response.

Two fellow soldiers who had been students at Clemson University in South Carolina before they were drafted went to Juárez every day. They weren't going for the leather goods or the copper but for the cheap tequila and even cheaper prostitutes plying their trade in the party atmosphere common to border towns. They invited Bayles to go with them often, but as a married man, he knew it was safer to go there with his wife than with a couple of single-minded bachelors.

"It was no place for a married man," he recalled.

With the months of training progressing and with Joanne feeling homesick for South Carolina, word came in July of the signing of the armistice ending the conflict in Korea. Bayles was in the midst of what was to be a six-month tour to be followed by two years of active service before a required six years in the reserves. But with the end of hostilities in east Asia and with the United States on the verge of recession, President Eisenhower tasked his secretary of defense, Charles E. Wilson, with reducing the defense budget significantly. Part of Wilson's solution including "rifting" officers off the active duty rolls and into the reserves once they had put in six months of service. The commissioned officers in the regular army would keep their rank, but reserve officers could be bumped back in rank, costing them their commands and a chunk of their income. Bayles's immediate commander, a colonel, was in that situation. He approached Bayles one day and asked what he could do for him. Bayles wasn't sure what he meant or why he was asking. The colonel responded that since Bayles was also going to be rifted out of the army and it would happen before he had enough time in to be eligible for a promotion to first lieutenant, he wondered if there was anything on the post he might be able to do for him as a thank-you for the job he had done serving him as his S1 in charge of personnel matters. As a commissioned officer, Bayles would retain his rank upon his transfer to the reserves.

His colonel added, "I can do it today because I'm a colonel today— but two weeks from now I'll be a sergeant, so you'd better get me now."

After some thought, Bayles asked to be made post athletic director and the colonel complied. In this role he was in charge of all post teams, fields, and facilities. He spent a lot of time in the post gym and had a Jeep driver who conveyed him wherever he needed to go. He thought it would last the remaining two or three months he would be at Fort Bliss before he reported for his permanent command at White Sands and awaited being transferred to the reserves and sent home. He also played some softball and baseball himself.

He was at the end of his six-month window by a few weeks with no orders yet to go either to New Mexico or to go home when he got the news that his grandmother, Ziza Young Mills, had passed away. Bayles and Joanne returned to Fort Mill for the funeral, and while they were there he received word he was being transferred directly to the reserves, his rank intact, and they did not need to return to Fort Bliss. Bayles's time in the active service was complete. He spent twelve years in the reserves, predominately in the Judge Advocate General (JAG) service. He worked with a JAG unit in Lexington, Virginia, along with a few of his professors at Washington and Lee while he finished law school. After graduation he joined the 12th JAG detachment in Columbia outside Fort Jackson. He was officially transferred from active to inactive reserves in 1964.

In 2003, at the beginning of the war in Iraq, he received a letter informing him that he was being reactivated and assigned to active duty. He was sixty-nine years old. Since he had never resigned his commission in the inactive reserves, he was still eligible to be reactivated. He called the adjutant general for South Carolina, Stan Spears, and asked what he needed to do. Spears told him he would likely be assigned to a JAG unit and that it was possible he could be deployed fairly quickly. He had just seen that happen to a doctor in a similar situation who had been sent to Fort Bragg and immediately deployed to Kuwait with the 82nd Airborne. He recommended Bayles transfer to the National Guard, which he promptly did.

After his transfer, he drilled with the guard for three years and was promoted to lieutenant colonel and eventually to colonel in October 2005. As of 2022 Bayles Mack is still a commissioned officer in the National Guard.

MACK AND MACK

Don't ever try a case unless you know what the outcome is going to be.

—J. P. "Spot" Mazingo, Darlington attorney

There was a rumor making the rounds that the bar examiners in South Carolina made a practice of failing first-time bar test-takers who attended out-of-state law schools. It didn't weigh heavily on Bayles's mind; he figured it was just a scare tactic and he was feeling good about his chances. At the completion of his time on active duty, he returned to Washington and Lee and finished his law studies, graduating on January 28, 1960, three days after the birth of his first child, Barry. With a new baby and a new law degree in hand, Bayles and Joanne returned to Fort Mill in February and he began preparing to take the bar exam.

He had taken the Virginia bar while he was still in law school and passed it, but he had never applied for a license in that state. With that success behind him, he thought he knew all he needed to know and sat for his South Carolina exam with confidence. Whether it was his lack of studying, the fact that the exam focus was not on federal law but solely devoted to state law, which he hadn't studied at his Virginia school, or that there was some possible truth to the rumor about out-of-staters failing the first time, he found he had been too confident and that he had failed on his first attempt.

"I wasn't a great student. I had learned to study at Davidson, so law school was a snap, but I wasn't a good student still."

Chastened by the outcome, he regrouped and went to stay with a cousin in Columbia for two weeks so he could study with students from the law school at the University of South Carolina. They were bound to have the inside track on a test consisting exclusively of state law. Two other hopefuls who had gone to school out of state and returned to the area were part of the study group. David White and Angela Roddy had earned their law degrees at Harvard and were now plodding through the whole of state law to take the exam as well.

Besides recent law school graduates, there were others cramming for the big test in anticipation of changes that were coming to state rules governing licensure of lawyers. This was to be the last year a candidate could sit for the bar after having "read the law" without graduating from an accredited law school.

The exam was held in a fire station in Columbia, and on his second attempt Bayles passed the test. His swearing-in ceremony was set for July 28. Billee was the only member of the family to attend the ceremony, but a fellow attorney and friend of Billee's came as well. J. P. Mazingo, known to everyone as "Spot," was a well-known lawyer from Darlington, South Carolina. He had a successful practice, primarily representing claimants in big insurance cases. He gave Bayles a word of advice that day that the newly-minted lawyer never forgot. "Never try a case unless you already know the outcome," Mazingo advised.

Years later Bayles would say of Mazingo, "He had the best law practice on the East Coast."

Mazingo had been elected to the South Carolina House of Representatives at age twenty when he was a student at USC and then to the South Carolina Senate by age twenty-four. He would prove to be a mentor of sorts to Bayles as his early career developed. He would also make an observation that day about the changing nature of politics that Bayles would remember nearly sixty years later. The swearing-in ceremony was held at the state capitol in Columbia in what was then the Supreme Court chambers. After the ceremony, Mazingo, Bayles, and Billee were standing in the hallway when a figure passed by them. Mazingo pointed out the man and spoke to his longtime friend.

"Billee, you see that guy walking down the hall there? You tell Bayles, 'You'd better watch that guy—he'll burn this place down like Sherman did.'"

The man was Harry Dent, one of the architects of what came to be known as the "Southern strategy." The South had long been the stronghold of the Democrats, dating all the way back to Civil War days. When President Abraham Lincoln, a Republican, issued his Emancipation Proclamation, it was the Democrats who opposed him and who worked tirelessly during and after Reconstruction to prevent racial equality. When early civil rights work in the 1950s resulted in the beginning of the wave that would collapse segregationist Jim Crow laws and eventually lead to comprehensive reform, Republicans developed the strategy aimed at appealing to Southern whites. It was pure racism cloaked in language crafted to polarize by demonizing affirmative action as unfair to white citizens. It exploited racial grievances and was the catalyst that led first to a temporary period where several states swung between Democratic and Republican control and later to the turning of the South from blue states to a virtually solid block of red. It was referred to as a "realignment" and politics in general began to take on a more adversarial and vitriolic tone as people became more divided.

The Southern strategy was master manipulation and an entire region continues to face accusations of harboring a racist ideology from the seeds of what was sown in this deliberate attempt to change the electoral map. Dent was credited with "articulating" the message of the strategy and he went on to serve in various political roles for many years.

Bayles, who would go on to a largely behind-the-scenes political life, himself looked back with a nostalgic view of pre-1960 politics.

"Politics were, I thought, a good thing. It was a gentleman's game. It was an honorable profession. But they made it *not* an honorable profession. When it was all Democrats, yes bad things went on. But civility was prevalent. When the parties started eating each other up, it became uncivil and the parties have ruined politics for the nation, in my opinion."

*

Finally an official South Carolina lawyer, Bayles needed a place to practice. During law school he had worked with attorney John Spratt Sr. at his office in York, about eighteen miles from Fort Mill. Along with his work there, he was also doing tax preparation out of his father's office beside the family home on Banks Street. His father would call clients and tell them, "Bayles is doing taxes," and they would come.

"The reason I was doing taxes is John Spratt was paying me $200 a month and I couldn't make a living," Bayles recalled with a chuckle.

He told Spratt he planned to return to Fort Mill full time and work with his father. Billee was still living off the sizeable inheritance from his father and had not actively practiced since 1945, but on September 1, 1960, a new shingle went up outside the Banks Street office and the law firm of Mack and Mack was born.

Bayles, Joanne, and son Barry had been living with Billee and Libba since their return from Virginia, but it was time for them to have their own place. Billee took a practical view of where they should go.

"If you're going to live in Fort Mill, you might as well live at Mills House."

The house that Libba's parents, J. B. and Ziza, had built on Confederate Street was available and no one wanted to see it sold outside the family. After Ziza passed away in 1957, some extended family members lived in the house temporarily. The house, a stately Classical Revival-style manor built in 1906, was just two blocks from Main Street and only a few blocks from the Banks Street house and office. Today the house is on the National Register of Historic Places and is regarded as one of the most beautiful in town with its columned porch and center pediment. In 1960 the house hadn't been updated significantly since it was new and in fifty-four years a lot had changed in more modern houses. Mills House had no heating or air conditioning, only one bathroom, and was sitting on pillars with no underpinning. Bayles remembered playing on stick horses under the house as a child. The asking price was $12,000, still a handsome sum to a twenty-six-year-old newly minted lawyer with no clients yet and a family to support. Bayles planned to cash in the stock his grandfather had left him and went to talk to his banker at the Fort Mill Depository about a loan for the balance. It was the bank owned by Billee's longtime friend, John Spratt. In later years it became known as the Bank of Fort Mill and was eventually bought and swallowed up by what is now the Bank of America.

When Bayles went to talk to the bank manager, Lonnie Abernathy, he walked into the building on Main Street with his father. Billee explained to Abernathy that Bayles had $4,000 in stock and wanted to borrow $8,000 to purchase the house. The banker was not impressed.

"He was proud and made people feel it," Bayles remembered.

"Billee, you'll have to sign his note," Abernathy told Bayles's father. Billee felt the slight aimed at his son and responded coolly.

"Lonnie, you make *him* the loan if you want to make it. If you don't, we'll go somewhere else."

And with that, father and son walked out of the bank. Bayles was convinced he wasn't going to get the money and kept asking his dad where else they might get it. Billee told him that he also had stock remaining and he would finance the purchase for him, but things took a turn before they had to resort to that plan. Billee decided to give John Spratt a call because of the way Bayles had been treated.

"Lonnie just scared him to death; made him feel like he wasn't a human being," he told Spratt. "I told him [Lonnie] I wasn't signing that note because he's trying to make it on his own," Billee told him.

It wasn't long until John Spratt made a call of his own, and soon Billee was on the receiving end of a call from a suddenly much more congenial Abernathy.

"About three or four days later we were back in the bank," Bayles recalled.

They made him the loan on his own.

"I don't know if we could have borrowed it somewhere else or not. But my dad just wasn't going to put up with that kind of treatment."

The Mills House was duly bought and the young family was soon living on their own. Eventually Bayles would buy the Elliott house next door, and the two homes remain in the family today.

Despite choosing a career in the law, Bayles never intended for it to be his only professional endeavor. Whether it was his father's admonition always to have other ventures in play because "you can't make any money as a small-town lawyer" or Bayles's natural inclination for business, it wasn't long before he was both practicing law and beginning to make the connections and the investments he would need for a lucrative parallel career that would include real estate holdings, a title company, a credit bureau, a finance company, and even a hotel.

A gregarious personality combined with a concerted effort to get to know as many people as possible in government and commerce made him a natural dealmaker. In 1961 Bayles and Buddy Mills, Harry Hallman, and Johnny Neal started a local chapter of the Jaycees, and Bayles was its first president in 1961 and 1962. The organization, founded to give young professionals the opportunity to develop leadership and management skills and to foster connections with their communities through service, had a big impact on Bayles, and a line from the group's creed has particular importance.

"Jaycees taught me more about government and community than any organization I've ever been in. There's one phrase that never leaves my mind: 'Government should be of laws rather than of men.' I think about that every time I turn the news on."

Later he would be appointed legal counsel for the state chapter. He also joined the Lions Club, another service organization, and was awarded "Lion of the Year" in 1968.

As Bayles built his network of friends and colleagues, he gained a reputation for being a good reader of people. In the courtroom, it made him a good evaluator of juries, and that brought him back in contact with Spot Mazingo, the lawyer who had attended his swearing-in ceremony.

Mazingo was representing the plaintiff in a personal injury case that was garnering a great deal of attention. He needed help from someone who was good at observing and picking jurors and at having a sense of what to expect from witnesses. His client, Janet Mickle, had been a passenger in an automobile accident that left her paralyzed from the chest down. Only seventeen years old at the time of the crash in 1962 and long before seat belt use was widespread, Janet was thrown across the front seat of the vehicle and impaled by the gear shift located on the steering column. The accident happened at an intersection in a construction zone where a stop sign had been removed. The vehicle she was traveling in was a 1949 Ford. Mazingo filed suit against the construction company that had removed the stop sign and also against Ford Motor Company. The automotive giant was accused of "negligence in the design and composition of the gearshift lever and of the knob or ball affixed thereto."[28]

Bayles was a young lawyer without experience in personal injury cases and asked Mazingo why he wanted him on the team.

"Cause you know the people and you read the jury well. That's what your job is. You don't have to argue the case. You just sit with me," Mazingo instructed him.

Mickle was awarded significant damages though appeals took years and stretched all the way to the South Carolina Supreme Court. Bayles learned a lot working alongside the elder attorney and watching how he conducted his efforts. Through the years, he would remember Mazingo's warning to him on his first day as an official lawyer about not taking cases when he couldn't predict the outcome. He took the advice to heart and made it his standard practice.

"I never did [take one]. Even when I was going to lose I still knew. And that's an ability to read juries, read communities, read government."

Asked how he was able to read these groups, he responded, "I think it's practicality and reality. And I read people based on that. Now, I make some bad judgments about people, but most of the time I don't because I see whether they're dreamers or whether they're realists. I want dreamers with me, but I don't necessarily want dreamers to be my assistants—because I like to work hard. I like people who are very practical because they're workers."

*

In 1964 the fifth congressional district, which includes Fort Mill, was heating up in a race for its next member of the United States House of Representatives. The incumbent, Robert Hemphill, had resigned his seat to accept an appointment to the United States District Court. Tom Gettys and Gene Coleman were vying in the primary to replace him. Bayles was approached by the Gettys family to help get the vote out for Tom, but Coleman was a cousin of Bayles's mother, Libba, and he was torn about getting involved when he had ties to both candidates. Eventually he agreed to play a low-key role for the Gettys campaign. On election night when the votes were counted, Gettys had won the seat and Bayles attended the victory party in Rock Hill. The Congressman-elect asked Bayles to consider coming to Washington to serve as his administrative assistant. He would run the office, hire staff, write letters, and manage relationships with constituents.

It didn't seem like a good time for the Macks to make a move. Bayles's legal practice was doing well and the family had grown with the birth of daughter Beth in February 1962. Bayles told Gettys he didn't think he'd be a good fit for the job.

"I don't know anything about running the office," he explained. "Lawyers are terrible managers and I don't know anything about that."

Gettys was not deterred. He knew he was going to be operating at a high level in an environment that could be very dog-eat-dog. He knew it firsthand because he had served as administrative assistant himself to another congressman and knew well what was needed. He told Bayles that what he wanted in his top assistant was someone loyal.

"I want you to do it. I know you'll protect me," he told Bayles. The appeal struck a chord with him.

"I thought that was pretty glamorous," Bayles recalled of the offer.

Gettys also told him he could do the job in Washington for a while and then come back home to run the district offices part time while resuming his law practice. Bayles and Joanne talked it over and determined the opportunity was worth the temporary upheaval. A family friend who lived in Washington knew the German ambassador who owned a house in McLean, Virginia, that was vacant. The Macks could move right in and they wouldn't even have to pay rent. Things were falling in line and soon the family was turning their sights to what would turn out to be a definitive experience for Bayles, who harbored his own political ambitions. The next stop was the nation's capital.

The Preacher: Joseph Bingham Mack.

Harriet Hudson Banks Mack.

The historic sanctuary at Unity Presbyterian Church. The bell commissioned by Joseph Bingham Mack still hangs in the steeple.

Bayles at age two with his great-grandmother, Harriet Banks Mack, who was ninety-three. They are on the porch of the Mack House that belonged to his great-grandparents. The tree grew up through the porch at Mrs. Mack's insistence. The photo appeared in the local newspaper in 1937.

Young Bayles with his mother at their house on Clebourne Street.

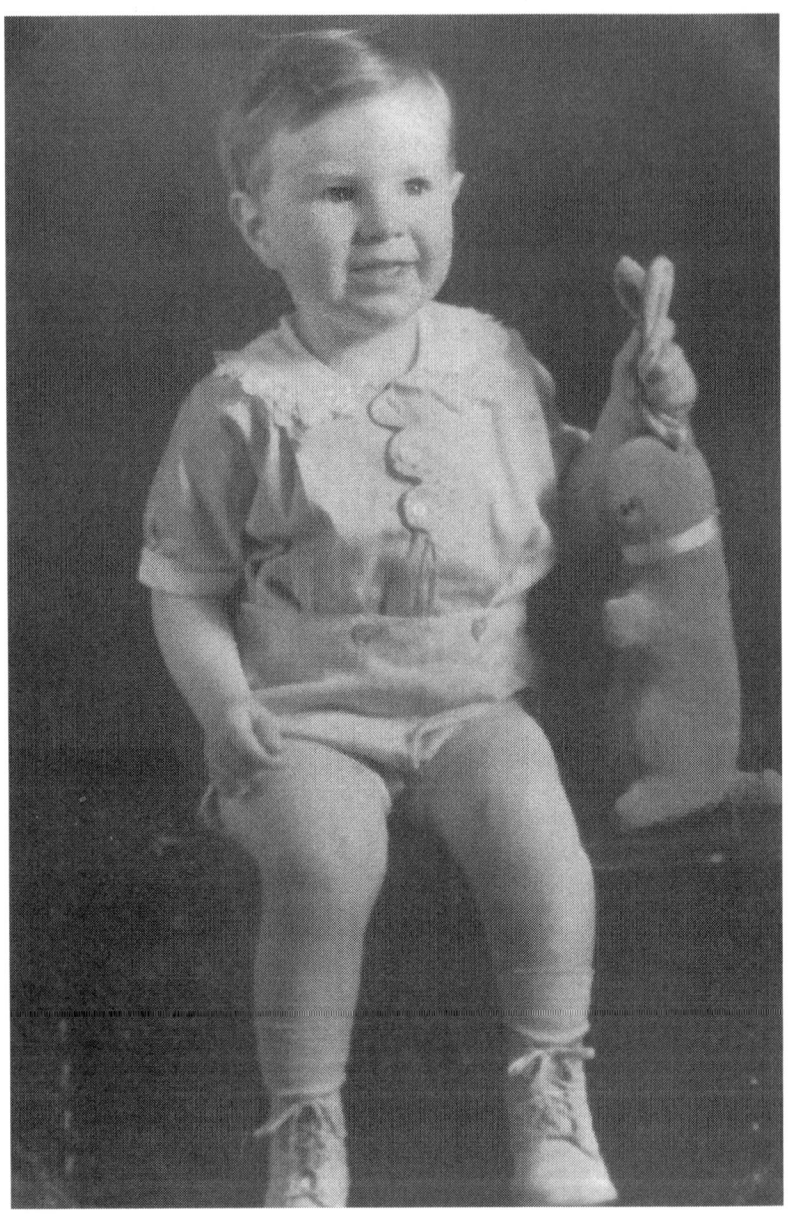

Bayles around age three.

Bayles at age four driving his toy tractor.

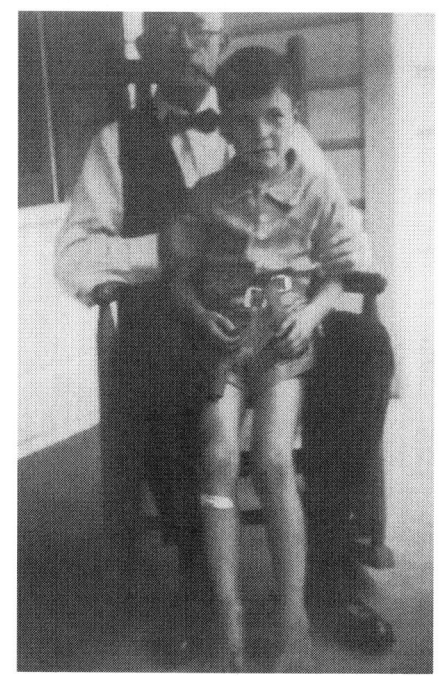

Bayles and his grandfather, William Mack Sr. on the porch at the Banks Street house, circa 1940.

*Minnie Bayles Mack, Bayles's grandmother whom he never met.
She passed away in 1908.*

William Bayles Mack, "Billee," Bayles's father the year he came to Fort Mill to be raised by his grandparents after the death of his mother.

Billee Mack college portrait with the signature "Just Billee" in the corner.

Ziza Young Mills, Bayles's maternal grandmother. It was to her house on Confederate Street that he would go somedays instead of grammar school.

William Mack Sr., Billee Mack, and Bayles in front of the Banks Street house, circa 1940.

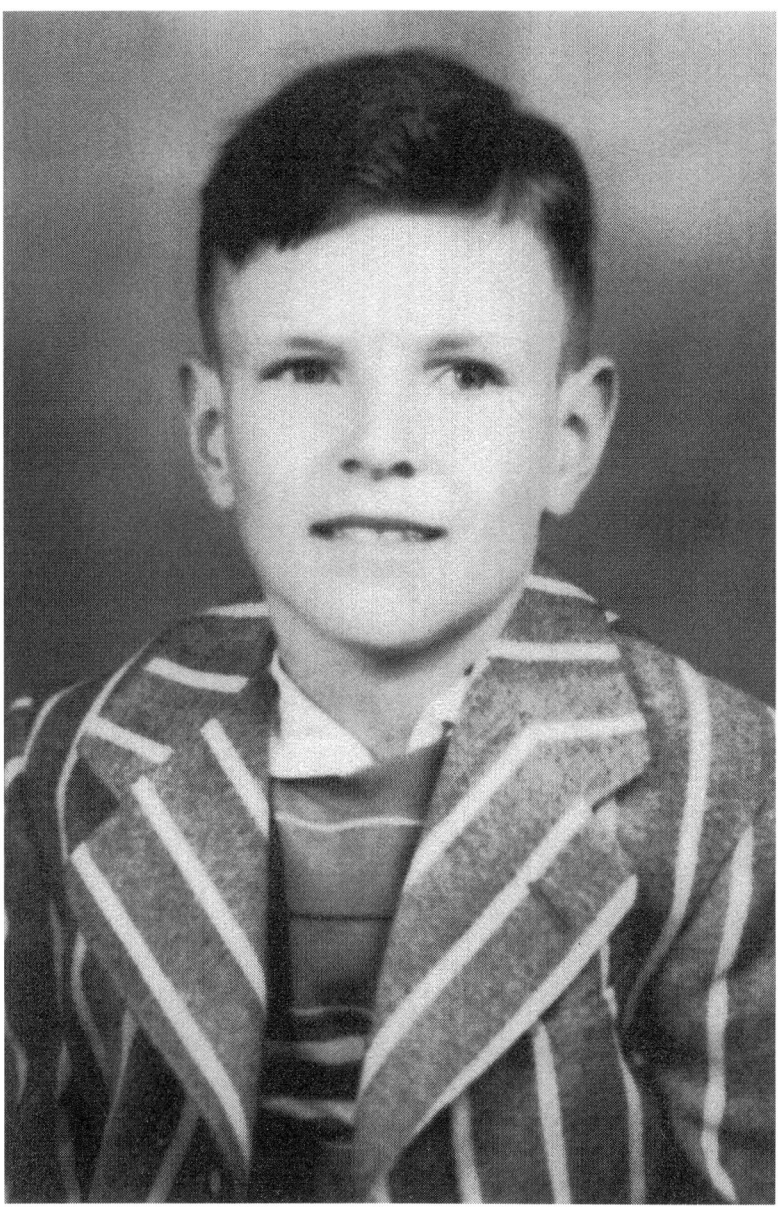

Bayles in third or fourth grade.

Bayles in seventh grade.

Bayles at age twelve in front of the Banks Street house where he grew up.

Bayles with his parents Billee and Libba at the Banks Street house, circa 1946.

Billee Mack and Harry Phillips outside Macks Law Library on Banks Street.

Bayles with his parents Libba and Billee around the time he started at Davidson College.

Bayles in his early twenties at Davidson College.

Bayles and Joanne Arnold on their wedding day, February 9, 1957. The wedding was held at First Baptist Church in Fort Mill.

Bayles while stationed at El Paso, Texas during the Korean War.
He was a second lieutenant.

Bayles in the law library at the Mack Law Firm soon after he passed the bar in 1960.

THE MACKS GO TO
WASHINGTON

*I have come to the conclusion that politics is too serious a
matter to be left to the politicians.*

—Charles de Gaulle

Few things can be as exciting for a newly elected member of congress
than the establishment of an office in one of the venerable buildings
that bracket the United States Capitol. They are connected to the
Capitol by underground tunnels, allowing for easy access out of the
weather. The tunnels are a veritable highway of staffers hurrying
to and fro, clearly on their way to do something important for the
republic. Interns can be seen ferrying constituents, children in tow,
down the corridors for private tours of the Capitol arranged through
their representatives' offices. There is even art on the walls and a

limited "subway" system so members of Congress can come and go from the chambers for debate and voting. The tunnels are an exclusive passageway invisible to the hoi polloi scurrying about above ground.

But it is in the offices of these connected buildings that members will spend most of their time and where they'll receive guests and take meetings. Some buildings are considered more prestigious than others, and proximity and placement within the buildings is a bit of a status symbol. Longstanding members hang on to their prime office spaces, but when newcomers arrive there's a process for assigning offices that can feel a little like assigning college freshmen to the dorm spaces the upperclassmen don't want. It's literally the luck of the draw. Freshmen representatives draw numbers from a mahogany box to establish the order in which they will be able to select an office suite from the list of those available by retiring or defeated incumbents. The best ones are snapped up by established representatives who trade up before the freshmen even get a crack at them. The rest are a hodgepodge of what's left. But the draw is not necessarily the end of it. It's the political world after all, and favors begin stacking up right from day one. After the draw, there may be maneuvering for a better place to call home.

Bayles's first job in Washington was getting Tom Gettys the office space he wanted. Gettys didn't have a particular space in mind, but he knew he wanted to be in the Longworth Building and close to an elevator. He was more no-nonsense than status-conscious, and Longworth was the middle building of the three. Being in that building and close to the elevator would allow him to walk out of his office and take the elevator directly to the tunnel, lickety-split.

Bayles made it happen, and soon they were in their new office and staffing up for the work ahead. In his role as the head of personnel,

Bayles hired John Little of Chester to handle agricultural issues in the state and Gene Owsley to serve as runner for the office. Owsley's job was to take around constituents who had come to visit their congressman and to make sure documents and correspondence made it to where they needed to be.

Occasionally it fell to Bayles himself to play tour guide. Gettys would often tell Bayles to take a group of constituents and make sure they got to go to see the places Washington is known for. Bayles had other staffers he could call on, even in other congressional offices, and sometimes he would arrange for whatever tour they were going to be on and make sure someone was with them. But when visitors went to the offices of the Senate, Bayles took them personally. South Carolina's Senators at the time were Strom Thurmond and Olin D. Johnston.

Johnston had been in the Senate since 1945 and he loved meeting South Carolina constituents when they came to town. He had an open-door policy—literally. His office suite in the Russell Building, as with most other suites, had a small lobby with a reception desk, but his private office was located just off the lobby and he kept the door open. Bayles remembers that before he could even get to the suite's reception desk the senator would call out and ask who he had brought with him. The visitors would get to meet and talk with the senior senator and it made their day, and often his too.

Johnston had once been a mill worker in a textile mill in Spartanburg and never forgot where he had come from. He liked to tell people his job had been to sweep in the mill, the lowest of all jobs. He would always thank the constituents for making the trip to Washington as the visit ended and then he would thank Bayles for getting them to his office.

"Bayles, I sure do appreciate you bringing them over here. I wouldn't have gotten to see them [if you hadn't]," Johnston told him.

His genuine interest in people from back home impressed Bayles. "That kind of stuff carries a lot of weight," he recalled.

Bayles would take the visitors to other Senate offices as well, including Strom Thurmond's and Teddy Kennedy's, but it was Johnston who always made time personally for walk-in visitors.

The world of Washington politics is in many ways a small one, and once again Bayles's personality and habit of getting to know as many people as he could worked in his favor. One of the early meetings Bayles attended was alongside the congressman when they went to the office of the sergeant at arms for the House. His name was Fishbait Miller and he was a good friend of Tom Gettys.

Gettys took Bayles in to meet Miller and said to him, "Fishbait, you take care of Bayles. Don't let him go awry."

Many people don't realize it, but it's possible to contact your elected official's office and request a flag that has flown atop the Capitol. Gettys's office would send out thirty to forty flags each month and they came from the sergeant at arms so Fishbait always responded promptly when the call came asking for yet another flag. He was equally attentive to other matters that fell under his jurisdiction.

While Bayles and Gettys were in Miller's office, a woman working in the reception area looked up and asked Bayles a question. "You're from Fort Mill, aren't you?"

He responded, "I sure am—and who are you?"

"I'm Carolyn West," came the reply.

Bayles's acquaintance with people from all over the state paid off. "You're from Chester, aren't you?" West responded that she was.

"Well, your sister lives in Fort Mill," he told her.

"I know it and that's how I know who *you* are," she said with finality.

She was Miller's secretary, and once the back-home connection had been made, Bayles had yet another friend well placed in the Washington establishment he could call on in his work.

His network of friends even stretched to the White House. Henry Hall Wilson was a fellow attorney from Monroe, North Carolina, who was then serving as chief of staff to President Lyndon B. Johnson. When Congressman Gettys wanted a group of constituents to see the White House, Bayles could just pick up the phone. It was an era before extensive background checks were required for all visitors and Wilson would often meet them at the gate himself and send the guests through with a guide while he chatted with Bayles. There was even a connection with First Lady "Ladybird" Johnson as one of her assigned secret service agents had been a classmate of Bayles's at Davidson. The relationships meant Bayles had better access to some places than even the congressman had.

"I called on those friendships and I could do almost anything I wanted up there and get people in and do things when Tom couldn't even do it." Bayles remembered the tone and easy cooperation of that time fondly. "It was a people-person kind of time."

Working for Gettys wasn't always an easy task. "It was hard work," Bayles recalled. "I hired, fired, wrote the letters, signed the letters, all of that. He was a taskmaster."

Gettys would get frustrated with himself and he often took it out on junior staff. As head of personnel, Bayles "was the defender and interceder between them because I'd hired them all."

Gettys would take him to task for hiring someone he thought wasn't doing a good job and Bayles would explain to the congressman that the staffer was doing fine work but was simply being asked to do too much. Senator Olin D. Johnston's sister even worked in the

Gettys office. Bayles and Gettys had a good relationship and he could generally smooth things over and keep the peace.

Nearly every Monday morning Bayles had a standing appointment at 8 a.m. at National Airport to pick up John Hardin and George Dunlap when they arrived from South Carolina. They were each representatives of federal savings and loan organizations and they came to Washington almost weekly to appear in person at the offices of the Home Loan Bank Board to collect the money they would lend out for home mortgages. They weren't required to come in person, but it was something they did to build relationships and to make sure their organizations were taken care of. Gettys wanted Bayles to attend to them personally, so he sent him to collect them from the airport and take them to their meetings. On his first visit with them to the board, he turned on the "aw, shucks" Southern charm with the government clerk who would be assisting them.

"Congressman Gettys said for y'all to treat these people right and by golly you'd better do it because I'm going to get hung if you don't and I'm here with them," Bayles drawled.

Hardin and Dunlap were able to collect more money than any other savings and loan organizations in South Carolina at the time because they were attentive and took the time to come in person and to develop the relationships that would benefit them.

In all these interactions Bayles was widening his circle of friends and acquaintances and building his network of people who could get things done. He knew his time in the city would be short because he had always planned to go back to Fort Mill and take up his law practice again while continuing to work part time opening and running the congressman's district offices. The move could not come soon enough for the rest of the Macks. The experience had not been a good one for them.

Bayles recalled, "It was a traumatic experience for my family. I was away from home all the time. Joanne did double duty. When I came down to the district every two weeks, I spent time in every county. We had nine or ten counties at that time."

All the counties were Democratic and he met everyone. He was so visible in the district that many people thought he was the congressman. Gettys noticed it and put it to Bayles, saying, "Everybody thinks you're the congressman because you go out in the field all the time." Bayles responded, "That's what *you* ought to be doing."

But they did get along well, and when they traveled together they "had more fun than a barrel of monkeys because he [Gettys] was such a character. He was straight-laced and very conservative."

As a new congressman, he would tell Bayles, "We're not going to file any bills this first year. Don't bring me any bills to file.'"

When Bayles asked why not, Gettys responded, "A freshman needs to be seen and not heard. Let's not try to impress our will on anybody up here. The best thing we can do is make friends and gather their respect and then they'll be wanting us with them." His approach worked, and he was re-elected four more times.

"He was a good politician," Bayles remarked.

Bayles's extensive work in the district, which focused around the three offices in Laurens, Sumter, and Rock Hill, gave him a broad base of support if he needed to call on it. His work in Washington and the connections he made there also added to a résumé that would look good when his turn came to run for office. While he was in Washington he took advantage of his role with the congressman "to make friends and make waves so I brought all that back here with me." The idea that he might one day succeed Gettys wasn't a far-fetched one, nor was he the only one planning for it.

A group of eight young Democrats from South Carolina working in various congressional offices on the hill formed an unofficial strategy group to keep tabs on what was happening politically back home. They commiserated on all things political and had a common interest— Robert F. Kennedy. President John F. Kennedy had been assassinated just months earlier and attention was already beginning to center on Robert as the family's next political hope. The eight South Carolinians, including Mike Daniel, Bubba Ming, Ken Holland, John Justice, Richard Sullivan, George Dean Johnson, Earle Morris, and Bayles decided they would take up the Kennedy cause in their state when the time came. They were supporters of the kinds of things the Kennedys were known to believe in as well, and it was a good match. The group planned to use their influence not only in their home state but also in the South as a whole.

A few years later, when the state Democratic party selected its delegation to attend the Democratic National Convention, all eight men were either delegates or party workers with some influence. They would make a name for themselves at that convention as a group of young renegades pushing back against the wishes of the older and more established state party leaders. Six years after that convention, Gettys announced he would not seek reelection for a sixth term. It was 1974 by that time, and the eight "young turks" who had seen their influence grow in the ten years since they were staffers scattered among the congressional offices got together and talked about who should run to replace Gettys. The vote fell in favor of Bayles because they felt he knew the most people and could win it. He also had reason to expect the support of the state American Legion, as they had presented an award jointly to Bayles and Tom Gettys for being friends to the military. The coalition of Bayles's Democratic colleagues would get behind him and help make it happen.

By this time, Bayles, Joanne, and the kids had been back in Fort Mill for several years and Bayles knew he had to talk to Joanne about making the commitment to run. A private person by nature, Joanne didn't enjoy the role of political wife and all that came with it, and the children were still young and in school as well. She told Bayles she would not return to Washington. He wasn't surprised by her response.

"I knew what she meant. I was always gone, and all the responsibility was on her. The kids were being raised, and Washington wasn't any place to raise them."

Bayles declined to enter the race and the strategy group got back together and determined Ken Holland would run for the seat instead. They all got behind him, Bayles included, and Holland won the election. The group would join forces again a few years later to support gubernatorial candidate Richard "Dick" Riley. They raised money for him and held campaign events in their hometowns to bring in sponsorships and donations. Riley won the election in 1979 and became South Carolina's 111th governor, serving two terms. He would go on to hold a cabinet position, as Secretary of Education, in the Bill Clinton administration. The "young turks" proved to be a powerful force in state politics.

Things were changing on the political landscape. Strom Thurmond, the longtime Democrat and brief Dixiecrat, had jumped ship entirely and joined the Republican party. In 1966 he was running to hold on to his Senate seat for the first time as a member of the GOP. While campaigning on Main Street in Fort Mill, Thurmond saw Bayles outside one of the stores. Thurmond had close ties to the Mack family, particularly Bayles's Uncle Murray, and he had also known Bayles in Washington during his tenure with Gettys. He called out to Bayles, and after they exchanged some pleasantries, the senator told Bayles he hoped he could count on his vote.

Bayles responded, "Well, you know, Senator, you and I have some big differences now. You've changed to another crowd. I'm a pretty staunch Democrat."

Thurmond motioned for Bayles to follow him a few feet away to a more private spot in an alcove and whispered in his ear, "You can be a good Democrat and vote for old Strom." Bayles chuckles when he recalls the exchange.

Thurmond would win as a Republican and continue to hold his seat, including a period serving as president pro tempore of the Senate, until his resignation in 2003, just months before his death at the age of one hundred. He had served in the Senate for forty-eight years.

Even before the opportunity to run for the Gettys seat had come up in 1974, Bayles's law partner, Palmer Freeman, had encouraged him to run for the state House for a seat that was about to be vacated. That would have meant being in Columbia a great deal of the time. Joanne had made her feelings clear regarding that possibility as well. Regarding Bayles taking up a seat in the state legislature, she told him, "You'll do that with your next wife."

Public office for Bayles would take on a different form eventually, but all of that was still years down the road when he and his congressional staff allies were preparing to make their first big foray onto the national political stage, where some of them would be delegates casting the votes. A new year was dawning and it would bring with it tremendous upheaval the country could not have anticipated. With his law practice and business interests continuing to grow, Bayles looked with anticipation toward what the year would bring. It was 1968.

CHICAGO, 1968

In all honesty, I cannot say much for the Convention and I fear the Democratic Party is in real trouble in South Carolina this year.[29]

—Lachlan L. Hyatt in a letter to
SC Governor Robert E. McNair

In a heavily unionized city like Chicago, transit strikes are not uncommon, but the timing couldn't have been worse for the city's taxi drivers to stage a walkout. The Democratic National Convention was about to start, bringing with it candidates, media, protesters, and the congressional delegations of every state in the union. It was an added layer of stress for a city already on the edge.

The tumultuous year began with the Soviet Union conducting a test of nuclear weapons on January 18 and with escalation in Vietnam in the form of the Tet Offensive on January 23. This action by the

Vietcong spurred stepped-up protests of US involvement in the war all over America and reached international proportions by March with an event in London's Grosvenor Square.

Race relations showed a marked decline beginning in February with a protest at a whites-only bowling alley in Orangeburg, South Carolina, that ended with three college students killed in the attempt by state highway patrolmen to break up the event. More civil rights disturbances followed at the University of Wisconsin in Madison and the University of North Carolina at Chapel Hill.

That same month, sanitation workers in Memphis went on strike to protest longstanding substandard working conditions and treatment of African American employees. The catalyst for the strike was the city government's response to the death of two African American workers crushed to death while on the job. In response, Dr. Martin Luther King Jr. had addressed a crowd of 25,000 in the city in March, urging them to stand together in non-violent protest. He returned to the city on April 3, speaking to a group of workers and famously telling them, "Like anybody, I would like to live a long life—longevity has its place. But I'm not concerned about that now. I've seen the promised land. I may not get there with you. But I want you to know tonight that we as a people will get to the promised land."[30]

The next evening Dr. King was assassinated as he stood on the balcony of the Lorraine Motel by a white man, James Earl Ray. Two days later, members of the Black Panthers ambushed police in Oakland, California, killing two officers.

In March, anti-Vietnam protests at Howard University, a historically African American college in Washington, D.C., resulted in the head of the US Selective Service, General Lewis Hershey, being shouted down by protesters chanting, "America is the black man's battleground!"[31]

In April, Vietnam War student protesters at Columbia University in New York took over the administration buildings and effectively shut down the school.

In June, with issues of race and with anger over the war in Vietnam now firmly intertwined, Democratic presidential candidate Robert F. Kennedy spoke before a group of supporters at the Ambassador Hotel in Los Angeles after winning that day's California primary. He told the crowd of cheering supporters, "My thanks to all of you. And now it's on to Chicago and let's win there!"[32]

Kennedy was escorted through the hotel kitchen, where he was shot three times by Sirhan Sirhan. The great hope of a large community of Democrats died hours later, on June 6, just eleven weeks before the start of the Democratic National Convention, where Robert F. Kennedy stood a fighting chance of being crowned the party's nominee for president.

In the wake of the Robert Kennedy assassination, a power vacuum formed and various factions sprang into action to fill it. Vice President Hubert Humphrey was the frontrunner, but groups began putting forth "favorite-son" nominations, hoping to inject new names into the race for the nomination at both the presidential and vice-presidential level. The effort to put Robert Kennedy's younger brother Edward (Ted), then a senator from Massachusetts, into the running got the most press coverage. Ted was thirty-six years old, barely above the required minimum age of thirty-five for presidential eligibility. The seat he occupied in the Senate had previously been held by another older brother, John F. Kennedy, the first of the brothers to fall to an assassin's bullet. With the legacy of a lost Camelot still fresh and the image of yet another Kennedy son cut down by violence, sentiment to see a Kennedy rise was high in some Democratic circles.

There were also rumors coming out of Texas that Gov. John Connally, himself a favorite-son candidate, might put forth Lyndon Johnson's name as well. Johnson had announced he would not seek reelection some months earlier after a dismal showing in New Hampshire, but circumstances had clearly changed. Back-room politicking was at a fevered pitch.

It was into this tinderbox that the South Carolina delegation, led by Gov. Robert McNair, arrived on August 23. When the slate of delegates had been elected in Columbia on March 23, a resolution was enacted that spelled out the procedure for selection and how their voting values would be assigned. Some would have a full vote, while others would be assigned only a half vote to make up the full complement of twenty-eight votes allowed for the state. Each of the state's six congressional districts would be allotted five delegates. One of the five would have a whole vote and the other four would each have half votes. The remainder of the state's votes would come from at-large delegates, including the party's executive committee members and other designees. Also included in the state's resolution was a provision that set the stage for the drama that followed: "The [South Carolina] delegation to the DNC shall on all issues cast their vote under the unit rule."[33]

Unit rule is the concept that all votes for a state be cast as a unit for the candidate preferred by the majority of the delegation. It was a long-held tradition at Democratic nominating conventions, although the action was technically governed at the state level. In 1968 there were so many credential challenges to state delegations on the basis they didn't adequately or proportionally represent the state's minorities that the move to abandon enforcement of the rule was made. Convention procedures like unit rule were later codified for the party by a set of rules adopted in 1972.

A copy of the state party's resolution of March 23 (that committed its delegation to unit rule) found in the archives at the University of South Carolina shows some handwritten edits from the meeting itself. Most are for clarity, like replacing "shall have" with "shall be." The line about unit rule was not in the original text. It was handwritten in its entirety as an addition in the meeting.[34] Since the DNC required enforcement of the unit rule on the national level, there was political cover to codify it on the state level. It cost the state no political capital to put a rule in writing that was going to be enforced at a higher level anyway. At least it seemed that way in March.

Fort Mill is part of the state's fifth congressional district. The original delegates selected were Ernest Finney of Sumter, George Gregory of Cheraw, Jimmy Nunnery of Chester, Glen Yarborough of Lancaster, and J. Lewis Moss of York. On an early list Moss's name is crossed out and replaced with John Justice of Great Falls. Participation in the convention is voluntary, even after a delegate has been named. Each is responsible for his or her own expenses, including travel to the convention city and hotel accommodations. Often a delegate will decline to participate based on cost or the inconvenience of scheduling the time away from work. For this reason, each district also elects a slate of alternates. They attend the convention and participate fully and may be called upon to vote in place of the five delegates for a variety of reasons. The fifth district's four alternates originally named in 1968 were Ed Burgess of Gaffney, Walter Brown of Winnsboro, John Rowland of McBee, and Bayles Mack of Fort Mill. By the time a "final" list of delegates was sent to the DNC in late July,

Ed Burgess had moved up to the main list, John Justice had become an alternate, and Ken Holland of Camden had replaced John Rowland. It's a bit tricky to keep up with the who's who because the full list of delegates and alternates appears in various forms in the archives at the South Carolina Political Collections Library at the University of South Carolina from various dates. Bayles's name appears on the main delegate list on a document received into the record in May that year although he appears on most lists as an alternate.

When the delegation arrived in Chicago, they checked into the Palmer House hotel, which had been assigned to them by the national convention committee. The convention itself would be held at the International Amphitheater with state delegations spread out in nearby hotels. In the evenings when the convention floor closed, they would retire to their hotels to caucus on the day's events and to consider strategy on the myriad of things they would be asked to vote on. From the party platform to credential and procedural matters, there were plenty of votes to be taken aside from the big one for the nomination. They had a lot of work to do.

Before the official proceedings began, the delegates had a chance to meet and mingle with other delegations at various state-party-sponsored social events. The South Carolina Democratic Convention scheduled a cocktail buffet to be held on Sunday evening, August 25, aboard the ship *Lady Lou*, which was docked in Burnham Harbor. This reception, falling on the night before the opening of the convention, was billed to Bradley, Graham, and Hanby, an advertising and publicity agency based in Columbia. The invoice for the event shows a per-person price of $2.75 for 200 guests plus $180 for a staff of seven bartenders, waitresses, and bus boys. The elegant affair would be the last bit of relaxation any of the delegation would get until they headed home to South Carolina.[35]

A walk in the park near the Palmer House revealed a virtual tableau of the active counter-culture movement. Flower children, hippies, and the "free love" crowd sang and drummed in circles and talked about achieving a peaceful utopia, eschewing material trappings, and the Grateful Dead.

In stark contrast, the walk around the convention site at the International Amphitheater might have been confused for a war zone. Chicago police, sheriff's deputies, US Secret Service agents, the FBI, and more than 18,000 Illinois National Guardsmen were on site, supplemented by 6,000 federal troops. Blockades, some with barbed wire, surrounded the venue. Soldiers outnumbered delegates four to one. The unprecedented security was a reasonable reaction to riots that had rocked the city in April that year.

After the assassination of Dr. King, major cities saw violence erupt in predominately African American communities. In the aftermath of three days of rioting in Chicago, which stretched over a twenty-eight-block area, more than 2,000 people had been arrested, nearly 100 police officers were injured, and 11 people were dead. Power and telephone lines were out of service and property damage left more than a thousand people homeless. Looting and property destruction, aimed largely at white-owned businesses, resulted in more than $10,000,000 in damages. By August when the convention was due to begin, Mayor Richard J. Daley was taking no chances with their level of preparedness.

In July, activists had filed permit applications to hold rallies at multiple locations in the city during the convention. They planned to hold events outside the main venue and at Grant Park and Soldier Field. They were granted a permit for only one location—Grant Park's bandshell. Undeterred, protesters began arriving in the city the week before the convention and took over Lincoln Park as their base of operations. Despite not having permission to be there, the protesters were allowed to remain in Lincoln Park, and police were ordered to enforce the park's normal 11 p.m. curfew in an attempt to establish and keep control.

The night before the convention opened, officers in riot gear descended on Lincoln Park, where a large crowd was still active at curfew time. The officers deployed tear gas into the park and then attacked the fleeing protesters with clubs.

On Tuesday protesters moved to the Hilton Hotel, where some of the candidates were staying. The National Guard was sent in to keep order even as protest leaders vowed to take up a position at the amphitheater itself "by any means necessary."

By Wednesday, when protesters met at Grant Park to stage the event for which the city had awarded a permit, 15,000 protesters were on hand and ready to move to the amphitheater, though they were surrounded by troops aimed at preventing their advance. When a protestor climbed a pole to take down the American flag, police moved in to arrest him and were attacked by the crowd. They retaliated with force, and the violence spilled out into the streets and back to the Hilton Hotel, where some of the candidates were staying. Innocent bystanders were caught up in the melee, and horrified Americans watched on television as scenes of brutal beatings and crowds struggling through clouds of tear gas played out on their television screens. The final straw ultimately had been the rejection of a proposed peace plank in the official party platform. It would have called for a complete halt to all bombing in Vietnam with attached conditions. Once word spread to the crowds outside that the plank had been defeated, the fuse was lit.

While the public watched the violence outside unfold, what was happening *inside* the convention and in the private delegation meetings regarding choosing a nominee was creating turmoil of a different sort, albeit in a more sophisticated and nonviolent manner. And a great deal of it was outside of the view of the media and the general public.

As the convention opened on August 26, floor battles had broken out over seating a number of the delegations due to challenges by the credentials committee claiming some did not adequately represent African Americans and Mexican Americans in proportion to their population. The delegation from Texas lost their challenge, while Georgia had two separate delegations fighting for official recognition and seating. As a result, the national convention conducted a floor vote and then announced it would abandon enforcement of the unit rule, allowing delegates to vote their consciences. This left South Carolina leaders without the political cover they had been counting on when they had resolved to hold their delegation to unit rule in March. It also raised the possibility that Gov. McNair's recent efforts at publicly aligning the state party's interests with those of the national party would be tested. South Carolina Democrats had a reputation for being "outsiders" to the national party. Accused of being part of a "Southern bloc" that could not be counted on to support the national aims, McNair was determined to solidify the relationship between the groups and had been quoted in recent newspaper articles on the subject. He had boldly announced, "The South Carolina party is now in the mainstream."[36]

With delegations finally seated and the convention formally opening, word came from Edward Kennedy's camp that the senator did not wish for his name to be placed for nomination. His statement did not stop supporters from continued efforts to "draft" him into the race. Such a scenario would put Kennedy into a sympathetic position with voters, showing his reluctance to capitalize on the recent tragedy and the legacy of two murdered brothers, while also demonstrating that he would pick up the mantle if it were thrust upon him. Kennedy admitted to the governor of Ohio that it was likely "the draft movement has gone too far to be stopped."[37] The absence of any gains that the heightened Kennedy mystique might bring left the Democrats facing a dilemma. Their frontrunner, Hubert Humphrey, was polling badly against the Republican nominee, Richard Nixon. Polls showed Nixon defeating Humphrey in the general election two to one. A Kennedy associate who was influential in the movement to draft Edward into the race was quoted as saying his nomination "could avoid what could be a disastrous year for the Democrats."[38]

The Democratic field had started filling up when Eugene McCarthy threw his hat in the ring the previous November, announcing he would challenge incumbent Lyndon B. Johnson for the nomination. Robert F. Kennedy had joined the race in March, and a dismal early showing for Johnson prompted him to announce at the end of that month that he would not seek reelection. His vice president, Hubert Humphrey, had immediately jumped in and was able to pick up the Johnson supporters. The timing was propitious for Humphrey as he was able to pick up those Johnson votes without having to compete in the primaries. Eventually George McGovern would round out the heavy-hitters vying for the nod. Now just weeks before the general election, the party was still struggling to field a candidate who had a chance of winning in November, and Kennedy supporters were gaining enough traction that they posed a real threat to frontrunner Humphrey.

On Friday before the beginning of the convention, Gov. McNair and fellow Southerners Gov. John Connally of Texas, Gov. Buford Ellington of Tennessee, Senator George Smathers of Georgia, and others identified what they believed to be a path to victory for Edward Kennedy in the delegate math. McNair was in a powerful position. He was chairman of the Southern Governors' Association and the National Democratic Governors' Conference as well as delegation chairman for South Carolina. The governors believed that if Humphrey did not get the requisite majority on the first ballot of voting, he would not ultimately get the nomination. They brought the scenario to the attention of the Humphrey camp, but his team didn't take it seriously and felt their lead was solid until Sunday, when the vice president arrived in Chicago.

By then, some of the delegations were getting antsy and the Kennedy backers saw a chance to peel them away from Humphrey. They were working hard to get McCarthy and McGovern to throw their support behind Kennedy to take the nomination away from the vice president. Once started, McNair, Connally, and the others believed it would create an insurmountable domino effect in favor of Kennedy. McNair, who had famously boasted, "There is no Southern bloc,"[39] just days before faced his first test much sooner than he imagined possible. As favorite-son candidates from their home states, McNair, Connally, and Ellington could expect their delegations to vote for them on a first ballot (in a move that would amount to little more than symbolism) so they announced they were giving up their status and freeing their delegations to vote for Humphrey. It was a calculated move, because there were delegates even from their own states who were expressing a desire to support Kennedy once unit rule was abandoned. Within the

South Carolina delegation, attitudes toward the vice president were mixed.

Bayles told a reporter from Rock Hill, "I don't mind the people of York County knowing that I am not an enthusiastic supporter of Vice President Hubert Humphrey."[40] He admitted that while he didn't support all the Kennedy policies, he did believe Edward Kennedy was the only hope to beat the Republicans in November.

All this maneuvering was particularly important to Gov. McNair for his own reasons. He had a good relationship with Hubert Humphrey, and supporters in South Carolina were behind a movement to proffer McNair as an option to be Humphrey's running mate if he won the nomination. For this reason, McNair had a vested interest in seeing his state delegation perform well for Humphrey. He envisioned South Carolina being the state that clinched the nomination for his friend and earning him a leg up toward getting on the ticket with him.

Having unit rule unenforced by the DNC wasn't completely without benefit for McNair because it could potentially bring representatives of the candidates to the delegation to offer the governor something to ensure they would get the votes.

"It gave the governor clout," Bayles recalled.

In response to those who might jump ship within their own delegation, calls began to go back and forth from Chicago to South Carolina. With the help of Spartanburg business owner and Humphrey supporter Lachlan Hyatt and his company jet, the director of the South Carolina Democratic Convention, Don Fowler, was soon winging his way to Chicago. Amid threats to "unseat" the uncooperative delegates, another plane left South Carolina carrying a replacement delegate loyal to McNair, and the stage was set. While the governor could not technically unseat a delegate, he could put considerable pressure on him and could replace him with an alternate. The players were aligning to give Humphrey the first ballot victory he needed.

Historically, political conventions and campaigning bore little to no resemblance to the system we know today. In the earliest days of the nation the vice-presidency went to the presidential candidate who came in second in electoral votes. Thus, John Adams because the first vice-president and so on. This system worked until there was eventually a tie that had to be resolved and until the country found itself with its two top leaders representing different parties. The twelfth amendment to the constitution made the two offices separate ballots in time for the 1804 election.

At the Republican convention in 1860, also held in Chicago, Abraham Lincoln did not clinch the nomination until the third ballot. In fact, Lincoln wasn't even present at the convention. It was common practice for the candidates not to attend and to stay home and wait to hear the results. Frontrunner William Seward had the most votes after the first ballot, but not enough for a majority. On the second ballot some of the delegates from another candidate shifted their votes to Lincoln and the vote ended with a virtual tie between Seward and Lincoln. Finally, on the third ballot, enough delegates who had been supporting candidates who had no chance of winning shifted their votes to Lincoln and he was declared the winner. His running mate was to be Hannibal Hamlin, but he was not chosen by Lincoln. The practice at the time was for the convention to choose the vice-presidential candidate, and the person holding the presidential nomination often had no input at all. It wasn't until the election of Franklin D. Roosevelt that candidates began choosing their own running mates.

Today the conventions exist mainly to formally crown the

frontrunning candidate and his or her personally chosen running mate. Though there may have been rumblings of a coup by faithless electors from time to time, it hasn't happened, and any drama surrounding the convention is usually drummed up by the media and unrelated to the actual proceedings. But in 1968 circumstances had conspired to toss everything up for grabs.

When the votes were counted on Wednesday evening, Humphrey clinched the nomination on the first ballot with 1759.25 votes. Eugene McCarthy was second, coming in at 601 votes. The vote count within the South Carolina delegation was unanimous; all 28 votes went for Humphrey. On the verge of potential mutiny, the Southern governors had taken action that would later be touted in an article in the *Beacon Journal-Chicago Daily News* with the headline *Sons of South Saved HHH*, referring to Hubert H. Humphrey.[41] Despite protestations to the contrary, it did appear there was an active Southern bloc at work after all.

A telegram duly arrived for Robert McNair at Palmer House from Anne and Jim Berry of Marion, South Carolina. It read: "We are proud of SC delegations dignity (stop) trust that Humphrey wise enuf [sic] to include you on ticket."[42]

All was going well for Robert McNair. Bayles told the Rock Hill *Evening Herald,* "When I went to bed at 5 o'clock this morning, McNair was among the top three possibilities for the second spot."[43]

But something changed that day, and by the convention's end on August 29, Hubert Humphrey had shifted his focus to the race in November, and the name on the ticket with him was Senator Edmund Muskie of Maine. All efforts to elevate Robert McNair to make him Humphrey's running mate had come to naught.

Whatever ended up happening on that last day is unclear. A letter from Governor McNair to South Carolina's US House Representative William J. Bryan Dorn dated a week after the convention includes this explanation: "I personally appreciate your willingness to fly to Chicago and place my name in nomination had I decided to continue as a 'favorite son.' However, upon sitting through the Monday evening session and seeing the mood of the Convention, especially the ultra-liberal groups from California, New York, Wisconsin, and others, all of us concluded that we did not want to be a party to locking up the Convention."[44]

While the governor was reporting to Rep. Dorn that he voluntarily withdrew from consideration after the Monday evening session, another letter he sent to R. B. Pamplin of the Georgia-Pacific Corporation, based in Portland, Oregon, told another story.

McNair wrote, "In the final analysis the Vice President concluded it would be best to name someone from the more populous East rather than the South. The decision was based on the uncertainty in many Southern states and the fact that he could get little assurance that he could claim at least four or five Southern states even with someone from the South on the ticket."[45]

The same day the McNair letter was on its way to Mr. Pamplin, a letter from Pamplin was sent to McNair. In his missive, Pamplin references three gentlemen: James F. Miller, president of Blyth and Company Inc. on Wall Street; John F Watlington Jr., president of Wachovia Bank and Trust Company in Winston-Salem, North Carolina; and John R. Beckett, president of Transamerica Corporation in San Francisco.

Pamplin wrote, "In keeping with the call from Mrs. Catherine Wulf, I got in touch on the phone with the following individuals and asked them to call Vice President Humphrey and recommend you for vice president." He goes on in the letter to say, "It was a pleasure for me to do this for you, and I am sorry it didn't bear fruit."[46]

Perhaps the rumors of a "Southern bloc" played a part, or there may have been other considerations. In the aftermath, the governor received letters of support and of criticism from state residents on how he had conducted the affairs in Chicago.

Donald G. Coker of Turbeville wrote inquiring if the sentiments attributed to the governor in the article about South Carolina being finally part of the national party were accurate, "for it affects many South Carolinians who consider themselves S.C. Democrats but cannot support the National party or its platform."[47]

In a letter dated September 20, the governor wrote to James J. Reid, commissioner of the South Carolina Industrial Commission, thanking him for his compliments on the way he handled things in Chicago. "I appreciate your most complimentary letter of September 6. As you know, it is not easy to take a position such as that taken by our delegation in Chicago. The state press is so controlled that it always tries to bring back a bad impression of us to the people of South Carolina."[48]

However events actually played out, one thing is certain; Bayles had been both witness to and participant in the most volatile political convention of the twentieth century, had toyed with the idea of defying his governor, who could have conceivably been the next vice president of the United States, and had come out of it deciding he was up to the challenge of national brinksmanship politics. Ever his mother's son and steeped in the tradition of good Southern manners, he wrote to Gov. McNair two weeks after the convention expressing his pleasure at being with the governor and his wife for the event.

"It was a memorable experience, and your presence there was a credit to our great state," he wrote. "If you are ever in York County, please come by to see me."[49]

In politics as in life, it's never a good idea to burn a bridge. Bayles Mack had not served at his last national convention. He would be back in '72.

BRANCHING OUT

*People think I know everybody. Now, I don't know
everybody and I know I don't know everybody. But I made
it a part of my profession to try to know every politician in
the state, every person that was over any agency, and any
person I was ever going to appear before.*

—Bayles Mack

After the intrigue and drama of the Chicago convention and before
the next round in Miami in 1972, things got back to a normal rhythm
for Bayles. In 1969 he took on his first elected position, although he
hadn't asked for the job or even known it was about to come his way.
The Town of Fort Mill had long employed John Spratt Sr. as town
attorney. Bayles had often attended the town council meetings on
Spratt's behalf since he was local and Spratt lived and practiced in the
town of York.

That year Fort Mill's town council saw an influx of new representatives. The only council member who was not new to the position was Bayles's cousin, Buddy Mills. He was the only member who had previously served on the council. The new members included another cousin, Ladd Mills, as well as Bayles's good friend Johnny Neal and a couple of employees of the local cotton mills, Monk Benfield and Gene Bolin. Bolin was a drinking buddy of Billee's at the Rexall Poll Hall. Fred "Hoot" Wilson, the son of the county supervisor and a teacher at Fort Mill High School during Bayles's time there, rounded out the council. Lunsford McFadden, another mill employee, was elected as the town's new mayor. At their first or second meeting the group took up the matter of electing the town attorney and clerk of council. The new leadership wanted to have their attorney be someone who would attend the meetings personally, preferably a local Fort Mill attorney rather than someone from a neighboring town.

After the meeting that night there was a knock on the door of the Mack house on Confederate Street. Bayles opened the door to find Johnny Neal, Buddy Mills, and Ladd Mills on the porch asking to come inside for a drink. When they had settled in, they broke the news.

"We came down here to inform you you've just been elected town attorney," they proudly informed Bayles.

"I didn't ask for it," he responded.

"But you got it," came the reply.

Ever practical, Bayles asked, "What do they pay?"

"A thousand dollars a year," they told him.

"What do I have to do?" he asked.

"You've got to come to every meeting."

Billee had always cautioned Bayles against holding any local office such as town council or school board. He said those roles would be "too close to the people and they'll give you hell every day. Get at least to the county level if you're going to run." But this offer wasn't the same as an actual council seat, and it appealed to Bayles's sense of community without the drawbacks that came with a traditional elected position. He may not have asked for it or even known it was a possibility, but he took the job and stayed with it for forty-four years. In fact, when he eventually did step down, his son Barry took up the reins and continues in the role today.

One of Bayles's first tasks as town attorney was to re-codify the town ordinances. State law required them to be continually updated and kept in a binder. The town had been operating on ordinances that had not been updated since 1945. Many needed updating and some just needed to be removed completely. One such obsolete rule that was technically still on the books required anyone driving a horse-drawn buggy on Main Street after dark to have someone in front of the buggy waving a light. That was clearly not a consideration in 1969, although why it wasn't removed in the 1945 version is a bit of a mystery as well. Bayles brought everything up to date, giving Fort Mill a complete set of ordinances that conformed to state requirements. They have been continually updated since that time. In an unfortunate twist, when the town hall was being moved to a new location, a clerk threw away all the old ordinances. Fortunately, Bayles had a copy of the 1945 version, so it remains for posterity.

When Bayles became town attorney, Fort Mill still operated under a council form of government. After home rule was passed in the mid-1970s, they adopted a manager form, but under the council form the manager of the town was called the "clerk." He didn't have broad powers, and part of his job was to literally take the minutes at the meetings. But he did have greater responsibilities than "clerk" would imply, and Bayles thought a stronger title would help convey stature onto the position. He lobbied for a change from "clerk" to "supervisor," "administrator," or "manager." The council decided to title the position as "manager." While still deriving authority and assignment of duties from the council, the stronger title was a benefit nonetheless.

*

Representing the town had to be scheduled alongside Bayles's private practice workload at Mack and Mack. But even with private cases, he sometimes found himself working for free. Before the county had a public defender system in place, the standard practice was for judges to assign pro-bono cases to attorneys and the attorneys themselves would try to work out a form of payment with defendants. Most defendants claimed they were destitute, so there was little remuneration in it for the lawyers. They could decline to accept a case, but to do so meant going in front of the judge to turn it down and that was an action best reserved for situations in which several cases were assigned and the lawyer was seeking to decline only one or two because of his case load. Nevertheless, it was important work and Bayles was often assigned such cases. A lot of them just involved showing up in court with the client to enter a plea. But it was never clear when a particular case would be called.

There was a jail cell at the York County Courthouse and a group of defendants would be brought over on Monday morning. Then they would settle in to wait for their cases to be called, and that meant their lawyers had to wait too. Sometimes a lawyer would have multiple cases, but time could really stretch on if you were waiting around to be called to handle just one or two.

"You could sit there a week if you didn't have but one," Bayles recalled. The time spent waiting at the courthouse was time he couldn't be spending tending to his other cases for paying clients, a tough reality for a young lawyer trying to build a practice.

Bob Hayes was a seasoned attorney and knew the ins and outs of the system. He became a mentor to Bayles in dealing with criminal cases like these. He started by teaching him a lesson about what it took to make any money with these largely pro-bono cases.

He told Bayles that when he came to court, "Don't bring your briefcase. Don't bring any law books. You come over here and you get you an envelope. You've got your stationery envelopes and you start putting down the name and the charge and you keep on going. When you get to the bottom of that page you might be breaking even. You turn it over and start the other side and when you get both sides filled and maybe some going the opposite way, you'll be making money."

Given that Bayles was often sitting there for days with just one case, it was a stark illustration of how upside-down the situation really was when you had a family to feed.

"You can't make any money that way," Hayes told him. But he had a solution. "I'll help you. You go on home, and when your case is called, I'll step up 'cause I'm going to be here the whole time. I've got every case here."

Given that most of the work was just entering a guilty plea, there was nothing else to be done, so it was a lifesaver for Bayles. Hayes had good reason for wanting to do Bayles a favor. He represented York County in the South Carolina Senate, a race Bayles's father had helped him win in 1956 against the incumbent, Lewis Wallace.

Billee had been Fort Mill's state Democratic Executive Committeeman and worked with his counterparts in York and Clover in a political coalition that effectively decided how the area's seats in the legislature would be apportioned. They were allotted four seats in the House and one in the Senate and the group determined Fort Mill would get two House seats, Clover would get two House seats, and York would get the Senate seat. The town of York was, and still is, the county seat of government. At the time, nearby Rock Hill had not grown to outpace the smaller towns in the way it eventually would. This coalition meant the representation favored the three towns to the exclusion of Rock Hill. It wasn't an illegal action, just a determination about where the time and money would be spent to get the votes needed. With the three towns aligned, Rock Hill didn't have the votes to overpower them. Republicans at the time were scarce on the ground in York County and in South Carolina as a whole. They didn't really factor at the polls, so wherever the power was within the Democratic party, that's where the wheels got the grease.

Bob Hayes, beneficiary of the efforts of the coalition, was a sitting senator when Bayles fell under his tutelage in the criminal court system, and when Hayes resigned his seat in 1966 to become a circuit judge for South Carolina's 16th circuit, Bayles again found himself working with him in that new role. Judge Hayes would hear pleas on Saturday mornings and Bayles and the other lawyers in the district would dutifully spend their Saturdays in his court for cases in both the Court of Common Pleas and General Sessions.

When Bayles was elected in 1974 to the State Democratic Executive Committee, he and the representatives from York and Clover continued the political alliance, but it was coming to an end. One reason it had been successful was the way voting was done in the state at the time. All votes were at-large, meaning there were no districts. Getting out the vote meant a lot of going door to door, attending local club meetings, getting people to the polls on election day, and standing outside shaking hands and soliciting votes right at the door of the precinct. There were no laws against campaigning right on precinct steps at that time. In the local cotton mills, company president Elliott White Springs encouraged his employees to vote and supplied buses at the end of the shifts to take them to the precinct—Fort Mill #1, the largest in the area.

The Democratic Executive Committeeman was also considered the unofficial ward heeler. It was his job to go get the votes that the Democratic bosses wanted. If Bayles was not to be found outside the precinct door shaking hands, he could be found at the mill gates doing the same thing as employees boarded the bus for the trip to cast their votes. There was substantial influence in the large precinct and even more with the support of the multi-precinct coalition

"We had a powerful box and we could make that box turn whatever way we wanted to just by talking to people," Bayles said. "You knew everybody there. I would stand out there and shake hands and say, 'I hope you help my friend so and so.' Sometimes people would outright ask who they should vote for on their way into the precinct."

During his time running the district offices for Congressman Gettys, he would raise "street money" to pay people to go out into the neighborhoods and give voters rides to the polls. The action wasn't without criticism by those who thought it was an unsavory practice, although it was really not any different than providing a bus to ferry a company's employees to the polls. Even Congressman Gettys had qualms about it, but he was safely ensconced in Washington and not on the ground in the district where the work of elections is done.

Bayles had a more practical take on it. "If you don't do it, you don't win," he said. Even today the practice is still prevalent, particularly in underserved areas of large cities.

With the growth of nearby Rock Hill, Bayles and the other coalition members recognized their three-way alliance couldn't continue to dominate the votes.

"You could see the writing on the wall. All you had to do was look and see what was going to happen and the voting was moving to Rock Hill so we had to be with that group."

The coalition would have to adapt, and adapt it did. New deals were brokered and soon the count was two House seats each for Fort Mill and Clover and the Senate seat for Rock Hill. York was out. Politics is a cutthroat business.

In the 1970s the practice of at-large voting would be replaced by districts, and the days of a coalition group having major influence were over.

"We've grown out of committee control. The days of having brokers in politics is gone," Bayles said he believed.

He extrapolated what happened on a local level to what happens with dealmaking now on a national level. "Now the power people are the money people and they use the money to make those same kinds of things happen. It used to be that you could be a worker in the mill and be active in politics and have maybe 300 or 400 people who would do what you wanted them to do and you had some power. Today the way people get that is money. They're buying it. Billions of dollars go to candidates to serve businesses, not to serve their communities."

Districting had another unforeseen byproduct—gerrymandering. "The districts were the ruination of voting and it is today the ruination of voting. That's what caused gerrymandering," he stated unequivocally.

Bayles's involvement in Democratic politics at the local and state level would once again see him called upon to represent the state on the national level at the next Democratic National Convention. Vietnam was still an issue and the push for women's rights was generating headlines. There was no marquee name on the ballot this time, but there was a controversial candidate, a virulent segregationist who had stood in the doorway of the University of Alabama nine years earlier in an attempt to block integration. In fact, history had almost repeated itself when the candidate was shot on May 15. George Wallace was not killed, but he was paralyzed from the waist down for life. Although it was unlikely he would be the nominee, he remained on the ballot and stood to exert significant influence due to the primary wins he had accumulated. The stage was set for another intriguing battle, and echoes of Chicago were not far from anyone's mind. But there was work to be done.

It was on to Miami.

MIAMI, 1972

I'm not a liberal but I'm not an ultra-conservative
either. I never have been. I always considered myself a
Kennedy-type Democrat. Benevolence is what I hoped I
accomplished anyway.

—Bayles Mack

On Sunday, July 9, 1972, a chartered DC-9 left Columbia bound for
Miami. On it were the members of the South Carolina delegation to
the Democratic National Convention. When they arrived in Miami
they would be shuttled to their oceanfront hotel, the Algiers, where
they would get down to the business of selecting the nominee who
would face off against President Richard Nixon in November. They
traveled to Florida having already survived a pitched battle to radically
change their makeup in the form of a challenge to their credentials
that could prevent them from even being seated at the convention.

The challenge did not sit well with state Democratic Party Chairman Don Fowler. In a May 1 letter to Lawrence O'Brien, chairman of the DNC, Fowler laid out the contradiction in standards between process and product created by the new rules and his opinion that the organization had never "defined in any degree of clarity which one of these two standards is paramount."

He went on to inform the chairman, while admitting he didn't expect a response to his letter, that "If the uncertainties involved in the delegate selection process make a circus out of the Miami Convention and we have a repetition of 1968, we might as well save our money and not run a candidate, pay off the debt, and wait until 1976." He ended the letter still ensuring the chairman of his best wishes and commitment to helping the party and stating, "The damn country can't stand four more years of Nixon."[50]

A full 40 percent of the delegations would be challenged that year, but South Carolina was the first on the convention calendar to be taken up and the outcome would be the litmus test for all challenges to come after it. The unprecedented number of challenges was a result of reformed rules developed after the 1968 convention. Ironically, the architect of the new rules was also the frontrunner for the party's nomination this time around—George McGovern. Now the very rules he had helped put in place threatened to undermine his candidacy as they drew the ire of the most vocal group in play that year—the representatives of the women's movement.

The reformed rules dictated how a state delegation must be chosen, requiring a proportional allocation of delegates based on population of minority groups in each state, elimination of "winner-take-all" vote encumbrances, and the assignment of voting powers to state party leaders and elected officials. This introduced the notion of a "superdelegate," who would be allowed to remain uncommitted until the convention itself.

Ghosts of 1968 Chicago were felt in the challenge to Mayor Richard Daley's delegation, and other states faced similar issues. But South Carolina stood to be the bellwether for the headline-generating women's groups because the challenge to its delegation was based on the number of females included. Nationally, the country was made up of more than 51 percent women, but the delegations included only 40-percent female representation. This was a huge leap from the 13-percent representation at the 1968 convention but potentially not enough to ensure success for issues the women's movement would be pressing, including the inclusion of a platform plank supporting unrestricted abortion and the push toward ratification of the Equal Rights Amendment, which had been passed by Congress just months earlier. The South Carolina delegation was made up of 25-percent women in its thirty-two-member roster, though the state's female population accounted for 51 percent, the same as the national percentage. Losing the challenge would require an increase in the number of females on the delegation from eight to sixteen. The political fallout that could come from losing this first-to-be-considered challenge might impact the convention not only from the perspective of the women's movement but also for the candidates themselves, depending on where they threw their support because a further eighteen states were facing challenges on the same grounds.

Frontrunner George McGovern had pledged his "unequivocal" support for the challenge and vowed he would stand behind efforts to see the delegation forced to alter its makeup. Hubert Humphrey, the Democratic nominee for president in 1968 and a repeat candidate for the nomination this time, knew a political time bomb when he saw one and took no official position on the challenge. Even so, those associated with his campaign voted largely against it.

Despite the fact that McGovern had good reason to back the upcoming challenges since it was his committee that instituted the rules, he faced a significant impediment to holding that line. In direct violation of the new rules, California had ruled its primary would be winner-take-all. McGovern had won the primary by a very small margin, and the 271 delegates would have been split among the candidates under his rules, but the state's defiance of the rules actually worked in his favor by turning a 5-percent margin of victory into a complete haul in his vote tally.

Georgia's governor, Jimmy Carter, had launched a "Stop McGovern" campaign aimed at splitting up the delegate votes in California, and more than one hundred fifty of them would go to other candidates if the move was successful. For this reason, the McGovern campaign had good reason to keep that from happening and it came to a head with the challenge against the South Carolina delegation. With fear that the changing demographic of the delegations if the challenges were successful could undermine his majority, word got around that McGovern's campaign quietly agreed it might be best to purposely lose the South Carolina challenge. It would set the stage for the defeat of similar challenges and hopefully keep the California votes intact.

On June 27 the challenge was heard by the credentials committee. South Carolina representatives argued they had made a "genuine effort" to solicit interest from women to become delegates, which satisfied the requirements of the rule. The challenge was defeated in a 70–56 vote; the delegation would be seated as presented. Later that same day challenges to the delegations from Alabama and Florida were also dismissed. Women's groups were outraged and felt betrayed by McGovern. Still, they vowed to fight on despite dissension in their own ranks. They would take their fight to the platform committee next.

Bayles was torn about the issues facing the party that year and his position on the plank caucus gave him an opportunity to hear the arguments firsthand. He came to the convention with an inherent affinity for the rights of women that he had learned from his parents. His father had been an early proponent of allowing women to hold jobs in textile mills outside of the office. The industry had long kept them off the mill floors thinking they would be a distraction to the men. The prevailing attitude was that it "caused confusion" in the mill. Eventually they were allowed into the profession and proved to be vital to the success of the enterprise. Whether or not they were a distraction to the men is debatable, but having greater economic freedom definitely had an impact on the women's domestic options. By the time Bayles came back to Fort Mill with his law license, women were on the job in the mill—and he handled one hundred divorces that year.

Bayles's mother, Libba, had influenced his view of women with her lessons on respect and the responsibilities of being a gentleman. While the Southern concept of "ladies and gentlemen" might seem old-fashioned and counterintuitive to the idea of equality, it didn't come across that way to Bayles. Instead, he saw the example his mother set of a strong woman, successful in the working world while managing the duties of home and family and taking up the slack where her husband's absence or drinking left a void. He developed a heightened respect for the role of women across the board as a result. He was also interested in using his political prowess to help female candidates for office and would be an early supporter of Harriet

Keyserling, who would make a tremendous mark on South Carolina politics. Keyserling was a New York-born Jewish housewife with a liberal political approach. She would go on to serve her adopted state of South Carolina for eight terms as a legislator in the state House and also as an activist devoted to reforming the "good ol' boy" political climate prevalent in the state. When she published her memoirs in 2004 under the title *Against the Tide: One Woman's Political Struggle,* she sent a copy to Bayles, inscribing the book, "You are the person who got me elected."

In the plank caucus meetings, Bayles heard Gloria Steinem speak for the first time and was deeply impressed with her. A journalist and political activist, Steinem had cofounded the National Women's Political Caucus the year before. During breaks in the plank caucus meetings, Bayles had an opportunity to talk with her privately on two occasions.

"She was a delightful person with a lot of charisma," he remembered. "She stood out like a movie star sort of person."

During one of their discussions she suddenly told him he was about to join her organization. "I'm signing you up," she told him.

He wrote her a check then and there. He remembers what she said when he gave her the check. "I don't know if it's true," he explains, "but she said, 'You're the first male member.'"

Whether or not Bayles Mack was the first male member of the National Women's Political Caucus isn't known, but he never forgot the experience. The convention was the last time he would ever see her.

By 1972 former governor and architect of much of the delegation's voting drama at the 1968 convention, Bob McNair, had a new role. He had been elected by the State Democratic Executive Committee to serve on the finance committee for the national party. It was a fitting role, given the former governor's previous efforts toward ensuring the state party conformed to the interests of the larger party. Under the new convention rules, he held one of the superdelegate slots given to state party leaders and elected officials. The others were Gov. John West, Lt. Gov. Earle Morris, US Senator Fritz Hollings, and James E. Clyburn from the Office of the Governor. Bayles was again representing the fifth congressional district, this time as a full delegate. Within the district caucuses he cast more votes than any other delegate, a total of forty-eight.

No longer tied to unit rule as a result of the convention reform rules, the thirty-two delegates were free to vote their individual consciences for the party's nominee and running mate. Though George Wallace remained on the ballot, his candidacy was effectively ended when he was shot earlier in the year. Sympathetic reactions in the aftermath of the shooting allowed him to increase his influence by mending some of the damage his past stances had done to his reputation. Still, he remained a segregationist at heart and probably never would have overcome the McGovern momentum. His value at the convention was largely to use his primary wins to leverage votes that threatened a first-ballot majority for McGovern. There were accusations that he was staying in not because he thought he could win the Democratic nomination, but that he planned to press his advantage as a third-party candidate. It kept everyone guessing, and that put Wallace in a power position.

The party's previous presidential nominee, Hubert Humphrey, wasn't faring as well in Miami. He had had his shot in 1968 and had not been able to defeat Nixon then. There was no reason to believe he could do it four years later. Even with his frontrunner status,

McGovern was facing the same polling realities that Humphrey had in 1968. The numbers didn't bode well for him to come out ahead in the general election. What he needed to be competitive was a strong running mate and not a single one of the potential candidates improved his poll numbers to a viable level. The man he needed with him on the ticket was Ted Kennedy, but Kennedy wasn't interested. In fact, he recommended other men in his stead. But the party being what it was and public sentiment still strong for a Kennedy on any ballot meant that there were factions willing to try and draft him into the race yet again.

On May 6, a column by Joseph Kraft appeared in the *New York Post* about the possibility of getting Kennedy into the race and whether it would make the difference for McGovern. In his column, Kraft reported a conversation with Kennedy in which he had pressed him on whether he would enter the race for president or for vice president. Unlike 1968, Ted Kennedy had a scandal under his belt now as a result of the death of Mary Jo Kopechne at Chappaquiddick in 1969.

He told Kraft, "If we lost they'd blame me. Then you'd never hear the end of it."[51]

Equally important, the specter of assassination still hung over his head. "There ought to be at least eight years between me and the era of my brothers."[52]

He was cautious and not eager to jump into the fray. However, as in 1968, his protestations didn't stop the rumblings that the party might put pressure on him because he could be the difference between a win and a loss in November.

A letter to Bob McNair from William Haddad of the United States R & D Corporation in New York City in response to the Kraft column illustrates the public view of party players McGovern and Humphrey.

McNair wrote, "I happen to disagree with Kraft. I think Kennedy would take a draft. I also think the surge of McGovern hinders it somewhat. You can't run the White Knight (McGovern) against the Black Knight (HHH) and expect to use Kennedy, after Chappaquiddick, to be used to stop the White Knight."[53]

Every angle was being considered in an effort to best Nixon in the general. With talk of white knights and black knights and playing one against the other, it seemed nothing was off limits.

Letters from Hubert Humphrey to Bob McNair show the candidate still had his old friend's complete support. On July 10, when the convention had convened, McNair received a letter from Chapel Hill, North Carolina, mayor Howard N. Lee inviting him to attend a meeting with a "relatively small group of Southern delegates to discuss a Southern Strategy and the possible formulation of a Southern coalition."[54]

On the convention floor various women's groups were lobbying hard for the inclusion of a platform plank supporting abortion on demand. With Roe v. Wade still a year away, the inclusion of the plank was aimed at putting national focus on a topic that many politicians had dodged by insisting it was a state issue. The convention saw its most dramatic moments when the issue, that supporters had failed to have listed in the majority platform and ultimately introduced as a minority resolution, still failed to pass and was not included in the final approved platform. Apoplectic activists screamed obscenities at organizers who had allowed a pro-life speaker to take the stage before the vote. Hollywood star Shirley MacLaine spoke out against including the plank because she didn't think it should be part of a presidential campaign. Feminist pioneers Betty Friedan and Gloria Steinem clashed on how to handle the issues, and activist Germaine

Greer later excoriated Steinem and others for failing to push hard enough for the inclusion of the plank.

"What reticence, what loserism had afflicted them?"[55] she asked.

Steinem was accused of settling for the fact that there was such an increase in female delegates and resolving to leave the issue of abortion for a fight down the road. Television cameras caught Steinem rushing down the aisle in tears. It was an ugly end to the campaign and a further sign that what had started as a women's movement years before had devolved into a splintered array of groups of varying degrees of radicalism who were battling among themselves instead of fielding a coherent single movement.

When the votes for the party's presidential nominee were counted, George McGovern had prevailed handily. His 1,729 votes gave him a 57-percent majority with his closest rival, Henry M. Jackson, coming in at just over 17 percent. George Wallace placed third with 12 percent, and Hubert Humphrey ranked sixth with just 2 percent. The first viable female presidential candidate, Shirley Chisholm, made a strong showing, landing fourth with 5 percent of the vote. To put it in perspective, she finished two places ahead of the man who had been the party's nominee just four years earlier.

Before McGovern could address the nation and collect his laurels, the matter of his running mate had to be decided. He had settled on Thomas Eagleton of Missouri, but in an action that bordered on the comical, the vote for vice president would be delayed for hours by floor nominations of candidates few people had ever heard of and at least one who didn't really exist.

By the time the nominations were done and a vote could be taken, there were seventy-seven candidates on the ballot. Eagleton prevailed with 59 percent of the vote, while Communist revolutionary and chairman of the People's Republic of China, Mao Zedong, collected 1 percent of the vote. At least he was a real person. Also receiving 1 percent was Archibald "Archie" Bunker, the fictional television character known for being a racist, homophobic anti-Semite.

The theatrics delayed the vote so long that by the time McGovern could take the stage to deliver his acceptance speech, it was nearly 3 a.m. Most Americans had gone to bed. The anticlimactic end to the convention was a harbinger of the catastrophe to follow. VP candidate Eagleton had to be dumped from the ticket just weeks later when it came to light that he had been treated for depression with electroshock treatment. McGovern scrambled for a replacement and went into the final months of the campaign with the husband of Kennedy sister Eunice, Sargent Shriver of Maryland, as his running mate. It seemed the party was determined to have someone, anyone, on the ticket who had ties to the Kennedys.

A few days after the convention, Hubert Humphrey sent a letter to his friend and ardent supporter Bob McNair. Without displaying any discernible self-awareness of his longshot status and ultimately poor convention performance, he told McNair, "To say the least, I was very disappointed that I wasn't able to do a better job. I still believe we could have and should have won."[56]

McNair received another letter, this time from Kenneth Calender of Rader and Associates, Inc., in Miami. The letter was written before Eagleton had been replaced on the ticket. Before addressing rumors that McNair would run again for South Carolina governor, he expressed his disappointment at the outcome of the convention.

"I still can't believe the 'whole thing'—a Socialist for a Democratic

Presidential candidate and a psychopath for our Vice President—how did it happen?"[57]

A letter from McNair back to Calender in August had just one line after the "Dear Ken" salutation: "Would you believe things have gotten worse?"[58]

To one of the state's delegates McNair wrote in August, "Although you attracted a lot of attention and voted in jest for Archie Bunker, we might be better off if we had nominated him."[59]

Clearly, there were many disillusioned Democrats in the weeks after the convention and their prospects did not look promising heading into November. At final count for the South Carolina delegation, McGovern had collected eight votes to Wallace's six. Bayles cast his vote for George Wallace and his vote for a running mate for Endicott Peabody, who finished fourth. Peabody outperformed Eagleton with the delegation two to one. The remaining votes for the VP slot were scattered among third-place finisher Mike Gravel and fifteenth-place Harold Hughes at one vote each with the final vote on the certified tally form going for Archie Bunker.

Communist dictators and fictional characters aside, the Democratic ticket of McGovern and Shriver would go down as one of the worst defeats on record come November. Richard Nixon and the Republicans held on to the White House, for a time at least. That would come with its own scandals and scrambling and set the stage for the Democrats to finally return to 1600 Pennsylvania Avenue in 1976. But that wasn't this delegation's problem. They had done their job.

The closing of the convention in Miami was also the closing of the chapter of Bayles's life that included the circus atmosphere and dashed hopes of national political conventions. His future endeavors would be focused in his home state, where he could make a real difference. Whether he was elected, appointed, or pulling strings behind the scenes, the coming decades would be spent where it had all started.

Bayles checked out of the Algiers Hotel and went home to Fort Mill.

BACK TO WORK

Bayles has lost thousands of dollars by taking calls and giving free legal advice. He's done that all his life. He's such a friend and he won't charge you.

—Harry Hogue

Bayles always had an instinct for making money. He took his father's admonition that he would have to be the "making it" generation to heart. While still in law school, he bought a cold case franchise for $500. Law students and practicing lawyers alike use briefs in their work, and those have to come from somewhere. In Bayles's case, the franchise he bought was a series of briefs done by Harvard students that they would then sell to other students. There was so much material that it filled ten lockers. Bayles went to work on the material, reducing it to a more manageable size and reselling it. He was pulling in $1,000 per semester, and when he was ready to move on, he sold the franchise for more than he had originally spent to buy it. Also, while in college he had worked as a liaison between the fraternities and a beer distributor. He was responsible for eighteen fraternities at Washington and Lee and seven barracks at nearby Virginia Military Institute. Bayles himself did not drink until he was in his 40s. While in the army, he had made the deal with the El Paso landlord that had kept his hard-earned military pay in his pocket and not spent on rent. These small endeavors helped bring in extra cash in his early years, but they weren't the kind of businesses that would allow him to make his mark in the long run. Those would have to be bigger and include not only his time and effort but also significant investments. After the Miami convention he turned his attention to finding new business avenues.

While he was looking for opportunities, he was keeping his law practice growing and continuing to spend as much time in public service as he could. In 1969 he began a two-year stint as magistrate for Fort Mill. In the South Carolina court system, magistrate court is the first in a series of court levels that hear cases of escalating importance. Traffic tickets, misdemeanors that were eligible for a fine and not more than thirty days in jail, and civil cases of $1,000 or less in damages were heard at the magistrate level in those days. Today magistrates can rule in civil cases up to $7,500. For felonies, divorces, child custody, and civil cases with larger damage limits, cases are assigned to the Court of Common Pleas, General Sessions Court, or any of their related branches such as Master and Equity, Domestic/Family, and Probate Court. Presiding as a magistrate gave Bayles a chance to learn a great deal about how things worked on the local level, and the experience would be helpful for the rest of his career.

The old method of having judges assign cases to lawyers to handle with little hope of payment was finally set aside by the development of a proper public defender system in the 1980s. Bayles's old friend Bob Hayes, who had helped him as a young lawyer struggling under the weight of pro-bono work, was instrumental in helping to devise the system. Once it was in place, Bayles was able to step away from working criminal cases and focus on other areas of the law.

With his law practice thriving and the credit bureau he started bringing in steady income, he was making enough money to begin investing and didn't have to look far for a place to put some of that cash.

Main Street in Fort Mill had been a thriving center for business for generations, but improvements in highway systems, the proliferation of the automobile, and trends toward shopping malls, supermarkets, and retail centers took a toll on small-town businesses all over the country. By the 1970s many of the businesses on Fort Mill's Main Street had succumbed to larger commercial centers in Rock Hill and across the state line in Charlotte and Pineville. Vacant storefronts dotted the streetscape, and the stores that remained were struggling to stay afloat. Bayles began buying any vacant properties, ultimately owning eleven of them. That's a large percentage of the properties considering that Fort Mill's Main Street is only two blocks long.

His first purchase was the fulfilment of the promise he had made in his high school senior yearbook when he vowed to one day be the owner of the Rexall Pool Hall. He bought the building (pool tables included), along with the attached office building at the rear and became landlord to the longtime gathering spot where his father had spent so much time. The pool hall featured arcade games alongside the pool tables by this time, and the manager would often bring Bayles the rent money in nickels and dimes from the machines. The building is the oldest retail space on Main Street.

He eventually bought out the remainder of three properties that had been owned by his Mills relatives after inheriting his mother's interest in these. One of these was the old hardware store, a place that had sentimental value to him. Main Street continued struggling for decades but began experiencing a resurgence in the 2010s. Today there are shops and restaurants lining the two-block stretch, and property values have increased substantially. Bayles still owns property on the street, including two storefronts that were combined to create yet another business venture, B. Mack Mercantile, an antiques store. He also bought property downtown that was used for parking.

When his train car was scheduled to be delivered, it required a large construction crane to lift if from the conveyance used to truck it to Fort Mill and then set it onto the prepared site. The parking lot he owned right next to the site was the perfect spot to place and operate the crane for the big move. The Town of Fort Mill wanted to lease the lot for municipal use and Bayles was happy to make a deal with them, but not until after the train car was in place. Setting up a rail carriage for stationary use wasn't an everyday job, and he wanted to make sure he had as much control over the immediate environment as possible.

It wasn't only commercial property that Bayles owned. Even though Billee Mack had vowed he would spend all the money his father had left him—and ultimately made good on that promise—he did own some land that he decided to divide between his brother, Murray, and Bayles. Uncle Murray and Billee didn't always see eye to eye. After the death of Billee's mother when he was a young boy, he came to be raised by his grandparents in Fort Mill. Murray, the younger brother of Billee's father, William, was still living at home and was put off by Billee's actions and how they affected his parents, J. B. and Harriet.

Even though the two were raised almost as brothers, Murray never had much use for Billee, but he was very close in later years to his grandnephew Bayles. It was Murray who had been military mayor of Seoul, Korea, when Bayles was in the army. Murray, whose full name was Francis Murray Mack, had the unique distinction of having served in four wars. He had fought in the Mexican Border War, both World Wars, and the Korean War. After his military service he spent his life farming around Fort Mill. Billee's father, William, had given him 190 acres off Doby's Bridge Road. Billee gave 158 of them to Murray. Bayles got the remaining 32. Murray farmed his acres and Bayles eventually sold his for residential development.

Outside of real estate, there were other ventures. Years before, Bayles had started a credit bureau in Fort Mill. It was the early 1960s, and instead of having three national credit reporting agencies as we have today, the industry was made up of hundreds of small agencies that would collect a monthly fee from businesses to belong to a local client group, and then the agency would provide credit reports to those businesses when they needed it. Businesses that were not subscribers could pay a per-report fee. The reports were used to make decisions about the creditworthiness of applicants before making loans or offering financing. When he started the company, Fort Mill Credit Bureau, Bayles brought his Aunt Evelyn Mills Merritt on board to run it. Before the business was started, local merchants had to go to Rock Hill for credit reports to conduct their financial affairs. Bayles carved out the Fort Mill territory for his company and serviced the merchants himself before selling it back to Rock Hill some years later.

Knowing which customers were good credit risks also proved to be important for another of Bayles's businesses. He and partner Ivan Chase opened Dollars and Sense, a finance company that offered loans primarily for appliance purchases. At the time, state law allowed for the full interest finance charge to be added to the cost of the loan at the beginning of the term before payments were made. This meant that if the customer wanted to pay off the debt early, the full finance charges were still collected. It made companies like Dollars and Sense a lot of money before the law was changed to subject lenders to regulation and interest caps.

Bayles would eventually be the proprietor of a title insurance company based in Fort Mill and a real estate agency at Myrtle Beach. But his most substantial foray into business came in a surprising way.

The city of Charlotte, North Carolina, and the city of Rock Hill, South Carolina, are 23.28 miles apart, and Fort Mill is right in the middle. Around 1970 a study was done to evaluate the hotel needs in that corridor and the results showed the area needed 825 rooms. Bayles learned of the study and looked into the feasibility of delving into that industry. He met with the Ramada corporation and managed to secure the franchise territory rights for a twenty-five-mile radius of Charlotte. The next step in the plan was to find land in the best location to build the first one. Enter Carl Latham and Jack White. They had land in Rock Hill near the spot where all indications pointed an extension of I-77 from Charlotte toward Columbia would eventually pass right by. The three men decided to form a corporation and settled on a name using each partner's middle initial. Mack and Mack drew up the paperwork and CIB, Inc., was born. Bayles and his two partners were officially in the hotel business.

Actually, Latham and White had prior ownership in a number of out-of-state Motel 6 inns so they had some idea of what they were getting into. But this was not to be a Motel 6. Even as the more upscale Ramadas went, this one was designed to compete with anything

Charlotte had to offer. It would have 130 rooms and a bridal suite, a 450-seat lounge featuring Las Vegas-style entertainment, and a French restaurant. Construction was completed in 1972 and the partners poached an experienced manager with excellent references from one of Charlotte's top hotels. Everything was in place for the money to start rolling in.

For a while it did. The bar alone brought in $10,000 per week. The hotel manager hired her daughter's band to provide the Vegas vibe and patrons dutifully ordered drinks and spent hours in the lounge. The problem wasn't the income from the bar; it was the losses they were suffering on the rest of the place. Low room occupancy and a restaurant that might have been a little too highbrow for the Cherry Road corridor were combining to dig a $25,000-per-month hole in their bottom line.

Joanne Mack had hosted the cotillion club at the hotel and reported to Bayles that she was embarrassed by the service they received. She wasn't the only one to notice. Rumors of poor service spread quickly in the hotel business and word got around. Additionally, Bayles's high hopes for the French restaurant were dashed by a lack of business.

"Rock Hill wasn't ready for a French restaurant," he remembered.

But if the restaurant wasn't sending enough fine cuisine out of the kitchen's front door, the problem certainly wasn't helped by the amount of food going out the back door. One night when Bayles was returning from a meeting in Columbia, he stopped by the hotel and noticed there were trucks parked behind the kitchen. He sat in his car and watched to see what was happening and then got out to question the chef. Large quantities of supplies, including expensive meat, were being carried out the door and loaded onto the trucks. Bayles asked what was happening and was told they were taking it somewhere to store it. In fact, they had been caught red-handed stealing the supplies. Bayles fired the chef on the spot but didn't turn him in to police.

The three partners had agreed on a $300 allowance per month that each could charge at the hotel. One of them spent considerably more on a regular basis, further eating into the profit margin. Bayles hired his brother-in-law, Jimmy Arnold, to be the night clerk so he could keep an eye on what the partner with the growing tab was doing and report his observations.

While the hotel was bleeding money, Bayles was supplying it to staunch the losses. At the time, both his children were in college at Davidson so the extra expense was a hardship on his income. He checked into the hotel himself to spend a few nights to evaluate the service and experience for himself. One of his discoveries was that hotel management had ordered an entire year's supply of toilet paper at one time. Still, the partners were hesitant to fire staff if it could be avoided. But with the losses continuing to pile up, Bayles finally had to take action. He brought in two men he knew from Davidson to take over management. They looked over the books and said the only hope for getting the hotel back in the black was improving occupancy.

The company held on to the hotel for a limited time, finally selling it around 1978. Bayles's idea of franchising Ramada Inns all around Charlotte was chalked up to a lesson learned.

"I never built another one because that one was such a disaster."

*

Over the years, Bayles served on a variety of boards, in service organizations, and with groups with a business or economic development focus. From his early involvement with the Jaycees and the Lions Club to his work with the Fort Mill Chamber of Commerce, his endeavors covered a broad spectrum of interests.

His father, Billee, had been one of the organizers of the Fort Mill chamber, and Bayles would serve as president for that group in 1963 and later as president of the Rock Hill chamber. He also served on the state chamber for a time. That organization is mostly a legislative lobbing group rather than performing the same functions as a local chapter.

At one time Rock Hill, Fort Mill, Clover, Lake Wylie, and York all had separate chambers of commerce. Bayles made a pitch to have the chambers consider consolidating.

"We need one chamber. We don't need five. We're spinning our wheels," he told colleagues.

He pointed out that employees would also be paid more if they consolidated and that much of the work would not have to be done by volunteers. He used his time with the Fort Mill chamber as an example.

"The president of the chamber was everything. There was no secretary. I was it."

He used his law office as his chamber office and had his legal secretary handle chamber business. Today the York County Regional Chamber of Commerce combines some of those formerly separate groups, although not every one of them opted in.

From 1973 to 1976 Bayles served on the board of directors for the Municipal Association of South Carolina, the agency that offers guidance and assistance to towns and cities.

Whether it was a result of a business venture of his own or by taking part in organizations that worked on behalf of other businesses, Bayles's career pursuits outside of politics and the law continued to show an interest in keeping multiple plates spinning. That kind of focus can take its toll on a family and on personal relationships. Over time he would find out just how much of a toll.

But as the 70s passed into memory and the prosperous 80s began, something not of his own making would strike his family without warning.

For the rest of his life he would remember the ringing telephone at 3 a.m. and his uncle's voice when he uttered a name that would forever separate the parts of his own life into "before" and "after."

Buddy.

MURDER ON STEELE STREET

He was like a brother to me.

—Bayles Mack

In his youth Bayles had depended on his cousin Buddy Mills to show him the lay of the land with regard to girls, sports, and social matters, such as when the time had come to stop being a prankster and start behaving like an up-and-coming young man. Buddy, whose real name was Gilbert, was two years older and Bayles and his friends treated him as if he held the keys to the mysteries of the much cooler and infinitely more hip upperclassmen.

In adulthood Buddy had shared some of the same interests that were common in their family and was elected to the Fort Mill Town Council, where he had been part of drafting Bayles to the position of town attorney. Later he was elected to the Fort Mill County Council, where he served two terms in the late 1960s. He was a Mills rather than a Mack, and that side of the family tended more toward business ventures than to the practice of law. Buddy earned his living as a salesman and was active in business organizations including the Fort Mill Jaycees and the South Carolina Jaycees. He was a Korean War veteran and was active with the American Legion, the Elks Club, and the VFW. He also had the outgoing, gregarious personality common to the Mills side of the family and was well-liked with a wide circle of friends and acquaintances. He, like Bayles, was active in Democratic politics and known to be a bit of a practical joker. His natural tendency toward social interaction often meant he could end an evening in his cups, having imbibed too heavily, and was known to conduct many a business meeting or relaxing night out over drinks.

In 1982 Buddy was fifty years old, on his third marriage, and struggling with a downturn in his sales career. He had recently lost his job with Clairol, Inc., and was pounding the pavement for a new position. While he was searching, he took a job with the York County tax assessor's office in June with hopes of getting back into the sales game as soon as he could land something. At his home on Summersby Street he lived with his wife, Shirley, and her three children from her first marriage: twenty-year-old daughter Lynne Gerald, eighteen-year-old son Terry Gerald, and sixteen-year-old son Kenny Gerald.

Besides a reputation as a drinker and prankster, Buddy was also known around town as a womanizer. Rumors of his conquests were common and he didn't deny that he had been an unfaithful husband. Buddy was Shirley's third husband, and that summer they had briefly separated. Her son Terry later told police that Buddy had stayed at the Bakers Motel in Cheraw for a week before he came back home and the couple reunited. Terry also mentioned that after they reconciled, Buddy started coming home late until Shirley complained and he made an effort to get home on time.[60]

Friday afternoon, November 19, Harry Hogue saw Buddy as he was leaving the old York County Courthouse. Hogue was the county tax assessor and Buddy's boss. After Buddy exited the side door, Hogue locked it and then noticed Buddy hurrying back toward him. He had forgotten his wine-colored jacket. Hogue let him back in, and Buddy grabbed the jacket. As he left he called back to his boss and friend.

"Behave yourself and have a good weekend!" Buddy told him.

"You too," Hogue responded.

The reply came back, "I've got it under the seat!"

Hogue explained, "That meant he had bought a bottle of liquor at lunchtime. But you had to understand Buddy. He loved to tell you things like that."

They were the last words Buddy ever said to Harry Hogue.

Later that night Shirley went upstairs to take a bath and Buddy called to her through the bathroom door just before 11 p.m. saying he had gotten a phone call from an old friend who asked him to meet for a drink at the Holiday Inn on Carowinds Blvd. Shirley reported that she had not heard the phone ring and that she told him, "Buddy, please don't go," to which he replied he promised he would be right back. He left the house on Summersby Drive at 11 o'clock. The couple had a new Oldsmobile in the driveway, but Buddy left it there and drove their 1975 blue Monte Carlo to meet his friend. The car had been in the shop for mechanical issues and had just been retrieved earlier that day. Buddy and Shirley had taken it for a drive to test the repairs and believed it was running properly.[61]

Summersby Drive is located in the area of Fort Mill known

as Whiteville Park. The neighborhood had taken root in what had been a wooded-area not far from the spot where the original town settlement was founded. It had developed as managers and higher-ups at the local textile mills built brick ranches and two-story homes for their families, and by the 1980s it was arguably the most desirable neighborhood in town. To get from Whiteville Park to Carowinds Blvd. where the Holiday Inn was located there were different possible routes. One of those was Steele Street. Largely running through a rural landscape dotted with peach orchards, the beginning of the street picked up in the Paradise neighborhood adjacent to Whiteville Park. The lower part of Steele Street ran through a section of Paradise with a reputation for crime before continuing on into the rural area. Out where it met the orchards it was a dark road with muddy pull-off areas where farm trucks could access the fruit trees. Buddy was known to have disliked traveling the road at night and warned his daughter and stepchildren not to drive through there. Still, that's the route he took himself that night on his way to a rendezvous at the Holiday Inn.

Terry Gerald arrived at the house on Summersby Street with his girlfriend Teresa Rister just after 11 o'clock. He noticed the Monte Carlo was not in the driveway and asked where Buddy was. His mother told him he had gone to the Holiday Inn to meet a friend. In an interview a few days later with police, Rister reported Terry had been in a somber mood that night and that he had been drinking, which led to his talking about the death of his natural father. Rister told police that earlier that year Shirley had been in an argument with Buddy and that while she was nursing her frustration with him, she came out to sit on the porch with Rister. After they had been sitting a while, she started to talk about her first husband, her children's father, Jerry Gerald. She recalled that the day Jerry was killed she was upset with him for "staying drunk all the time."[62] She relayed to Rister that she had told him to "Get off his tail and cut the grass."[63] He left the house to buy gas and was killed in a fiery automobile crash while on that errand. Terry was recalling the event of his father's death that Friday night before settling down to watch television. Rister's statement said that around 12:30 a.m. Terry's sister, Lynne, got home and a few minutes later Terry left the house to drive her (Rister) home.[64]

Lynne had worked a restaurant shift at Rigby's in Charlotte that evening, clocking out around 10:30 and then hanging around a bit longer to eat dinner and chat with friends. After she left, she drove to her boyfriend's house on Laurel Circle in Whiteville Park. On the way, she had driven down Steele Street and noticed the Monte Carlo on the side of the road and thought it had broken down, but she didn't see anyone in the car so she continued on. She later told police that Buddy had warned her against traveling that road and that she had done it only one other time before that night. After spending some time at her boyfriend's house, she got home around 12:30.

While Rister had reported being at the house when Lynne got there, Lynne reported she arrived at home to find the television on but nobody in the room. She told police she thought her brother had taken the Monte Carlo and that it had broken down on him since he had driven the car in the past. Lynne went to find her mother to tell her about the car and Shirley told her Buddy had taken it to go meet a friend after receiving a call around 10:50 that night. When Lynne saw the car, it was pointed in the direction of Carowinds Blvd., leading her to mention to her mother that she didn't think Buddy had made it to the hotel. Lynne played cards while her mother made a call in the other room and then she went to bed.[65]

The call Shirley placed was to Buddy's brother, Ladd Mills. She told him Lynne had arrived home and reported seeing the Monte Carlo on the side of Steele Street. She asked Ladd to go check on Buddy. It was just before 1 o'clock on Saturday morning.[66]

Ladd Mills left his house on Spratt Street and arrived beside the Monte Carlo at 1:10. He noticed that both doors were closed and the parking lights were on. He opened the driver's door to find his brother slumped in the seat and leaning toward the passenger side. He saw blood and felt Buddy's arm. He believed he was dead and closed the door before driving to Fort Mill Police headquarters. Officer Jack McKinney returned to the scene with Mills. The officer called for the rescue squad to meet them and also put out a call for York County Sheriff's officers to respond since the scene was actually not within Fort Mill town limits. The South Carolina Law Enforcement Division, SLED, dispatched an agent to the scene as well. The rescue squad arrived at 1:18 and, finding no vital signs, closed the car and waited for investigators. As officers from the sheriff's department arrived on the scene, they took photos and noted their impressions.[67]

A Deputy Giles submitted a detailed report of his observations. "There was a wound to the back that appeared to be in the neck area. The victim had one foot on the gas pedal and the other to the left side of the brake pedal. The car's parking lights were on. The ignition was turned off, but not in a lock position. Both doors were unlocked but shut. The driver's side window was down about ten inches."[68]

His report went on to describe the gruesome scene inside the car.

"There was an area of blood about eighteen inches long and about three inches wide from the rear of the passenger door and back. There was a puddle of blood in the floor in the back behind the passenger seat. Blood was splattered along the front dash and rear seat. There were torn places in the front dash that appeared to have been where pellets struck, and the front windshield had at least one crack. Blood was also smeared across the passenger seat."[69]

Another report notes that the car appears to have continued moving several yards from the location of where it may have initially been sitting. There was a build-up of mud behind, indicating tires had spun at a high rate of speed and that the car had come to rest some distance away. There were also footprints in the mud. Coroner Cotton Howell oversaw the removal of the body and ordered it transferred to York General Hospital in Rock Hill, where an autopsy was scheduled for the next morning. The car was towed to the York County Detention Center and stored in the old sally port for processing.[70]

The following morning Dr. James Maynard began the autopsy. He recovered a number of items from the body during the preparation phase. An inventory lists one man's gold Seiko watch, one man's gold wedding band, one black billfold with assorted credit cards and the victim's South Carolina driver's license, $50 in cash (broken down by denomination), and seven plastic sticks "used for mixed drinks."[71]

The next phase yielded another list of items collected, these to be retained by law enforcement as evidence. The list outlined everything Buddy had been wearing right down to the sizes and manufacturer of each garment. One item stuck out, particularly because it appears on this list and not on the earlier list of items found in his pockets. The detailed clothing list, itemized as A through G, also includes this line: "H-ONE ROLL 35 mm FILM."[72] There is no reference anywhere in the file as to what happened to that roll of film.

The final list from the autopsy report includes four items, listed as A through D. One is a hair found on the victim and the other three are detailed descriptions of the shotgun pellets and wadding found in the body and the location of each.[73]

The findings were official: Gilbert "Buddy" Mills, age fifty, was dead of a close-range shotgun blast to the rear of the neck. The doctor told Chief Deputy Gene Ervin that the wound had damaged the spinal cord and would have resulted in not only instant loss of all muscle control but also likely instant death. The victim was still wearing his gold jewelry, and his cash and credit cards were still in his wallet. He had not been robbed. He was traveling a road he was known to avoid and had never made it to the Holiday Inn. Was he actually going there at all? He had been so vocal about telling people not to use Steele Street after dark that the Rock Hill *Evening Herald* used it as a headline on a November 23 article about the crime. "Mills disliked road where he was killed" jumped out from page 16.[74]

Witness statements collected over the next few weeks would include several people who reportedly saw the car running with the dome light on and Buddy visible inside for a time and others seeing it after it had moved up the road and the engine was turned to the accessory position and the car only had its parking lights on. By all accounts, Buddy had pulled over on the side of the road and had his window rolled partially down when he was shot. Add that to Shirley Mills's report that she had never heard ringing for the supposed call that Buddy said had come in prior to 11 p.m. She hadn't heard a call despite there being three phones in the house, one not far from the bathroom where she was taking a bath.[75] Had there been a call to Buddy at all, and if not, why did he leave the house? The question that was nagging investigators was a simple one. "What was he doing there on the side of that road?"

In the hours after the murder while investigators were still at the scene, word began to spread to family members. Ladd Mills had shown up at the house on Summersby and broken the news to Shirley around 2 a.m.

Buddy's only child, twenty-four-year-old daughter Barbara, known as Gigi, was notified shortly thereafter. Gigi had just finished graduate school and was living in Charlotte and working as an accountant. Two weeks before, she had visited her father at home and would later tell police she found him to be in a better mood than she had seen him since he had lost his job. After he and Shirley married, she and her three children moved into the house on Summersby where Gigi had grown up. By that time she was away at college, but Buddy made sure to preserve her room for her use whenever she was home. Nearly thirty-seven years after the murder, Gigi recalled her relationship with her stepmother, saying, "Shirley was always kind to me." The relationship between Gigi and Buddy's new family was a good one.

In Gigi's statement to police on November 24, she too noted that her father had told her not to use Steele Street when she was out driving. Even years later, she remembered how adamant he had been about it.[76]

"He absolutely forbade it," she recalled.

On the weekend of her father's death, Gigi had traveled to Charleston to visit a friend from high school. Her Uncle Ladd knew she was visiting there and called his son, also named Ladson, an Episcopal priest living in Charleston. Ladson was known by a nickname as well, "Punchy." Ladd and Punchy put their heads together to recall the married name of Gigi's friend and Punchy was able to track down her phone number. He broke the news to Gigi, who fainted on the spot. Punchy went to the house where she was staying and absolutely refused to entertain the idea of her driving the three hours home alone. He got a plane ticket for her for the next morning. She flew back to Charlotte and Punchy followed with her car.

The phone rang at Bayles and Joanne's house at 3 o'clock. It was Ladd. Upon hearing Buddy was dead, Bayles asked if there had been a car accident. He was surprised when the response came that the man who had been like a brother to him had been shot. He woke Joanne and they drove over to the house, where they found a stoic Shirley sitting in the living room. Others continued to arrive throughout the night to keep vigil and speculate on what could have happened. After a while at Buddy's house, Bayles and Joanne got ready to leave to go break the news to his mother, Libba, and his Aunt Evelyn.

Later as he prepared to leave his mother's house, he told her he planned to go to the sheriff's department on Monday morning to find out what he could. Cryptically his mother warned him against getting involved.

"Bayles, don't you go. They know how close you were to Buddy and they'll get you too," she told him. Whoever, "they" were wasn't clear, but with no idea of what had happened, the family was understandably uneasy.

Over the next weeks and months, witness interviews would be conducted and the investigation would spread to a number of persons of interest both inside and outside of York County. Chief Deputy Gene Ervin accompanied Shirley Mills to Columbia shortly after the murder so she could take a polygraph exam. York County did not have polygraph capability at the time. The results were inconclusive because she had been given medication in the aftermath of the murder. She was never asked to submit to a second test.

Others were polygraphed, most in Columbia, but the case file included one polygraph report that was done on a man in Gaston

County, North Carolina. He responded to the investigator's questions indicating he had met with a woman in York County and discussed the possibility of committing a homicide for her. He responded "yes" to a question about whether or not the crime they discussed had been carried out.[77] The polygraph was administered on December 29, five weeks after the murder. The man's name does not appear anywhere else in the case file, so police apparently did not believe him to be a credible witness.

Two composite sketches were done of a man who was reportedly driving up and down Unity Street the evening of the murder before stopping to ask two locals who were out for a walk how to get to Steele Street. He had stopped to talk with them on his third pass down the street between 7:00 and 8:00 p.m. One sketch was computer-generated and done by the Charlotte Police Department just three days after the murder and under the supervision of one of their homicide detectives. Eight months later, the same witness was asked to cooperate with a hypnosis expert to develop a second composite. Using the Identi-Kit Model II, a sketch was made in consultation with the witness while he was under hypnosis at the practitioner's office in Columbia. The two sketches, made months apart by different methods, are significantly different in appearance.

Buddy's reported infidelities provided another avenue for suspicion. Shirley reported to police that she had received a phone call over the summer asking if she knew her husband was having an affair with a woman in Rock Hill. Police interviewed the woman, who reported that she and Buddy had been in a relationship before he met Shirley but that they had not been involved in an extra-marital affair. The names of other women were batted about and police followed up, finding no leads. Speaking thirty-seven years after the murder, Chief

Deputy Ervin recalled the rumor mill around town at that time being filled with comments like "Wonder which one of the husbands did it?" Despite the rumors, there was no evidence to support the theory of a disgruntled husband taking revenge.

Spouses are always first on an investigator's list whether there is any reason to be suspicious or not. Almost immediately after the murder, Fort Mill Police received an anonymous phone call encouraging them to look into Shirley because of the circumstances surrounding the death of her first husband, Jerry Gerald, on March 31, 1972. His death while running an errand to get gas in order to mow the lawn had been the result of a fiery crash. York County investigators contacted Bernard Stubbs, who had been the coroner in Chesterfield County at the time of the death. He reported that a call had come in to their sheriff's office about a car burning in a ditch eight miles outside of Cheraw. Gerald had burned to death in his 1970 Ford Maverick and coroner Stubbs reported the death was ruled accidental. He said Gerald was an alcoholic who had been out all night the previous evening and that on his errand to get gas he was believed to have lit a cigarette in the car, implying he had purchased the gasoline and had the can inside the car. Stubbs told York County investigators that he believed Shirley had nothing to do with Jerry's death.[78]

Anonymous tips often turn out to be dead-ends or even grudge-related fiction. After the death of Jerry, Shirley married a second time, this time to Frank Royce Sherrill. By the time of Buddy's murder in 1982, Sherrill was already a suspect in a 1979 bombing of a local attorney's car in Cheraw. Court orders were issued to obtain long-distance phone records for several numbers in Cheraw, including residences as well as the Pace Service Station and Cheraw Airport. They also requested the records for the two landlines that were in

Buddy and Shirley's home. In addition to the main number, there was a separate line for the children. Records showed multiple calls to and from the locations in question in Cheraw and the Mills house. Most were on the main number, but some were to the children's line. Before long, Sherrill topped a shortlist of persons of interest. The list also included Fort Mill residents Elam and Sarah Kathrine Gray. On December 1 Fort Mill Chief of Police Bobby Kimble reported to York County investigators that a witness had contacted him and reported seeing Buddy pull off Steele Street onto a dirt road leading into the peach orchard, followed by a Chevrolet station wagon driven by a white female with a ponytail. This was six weeks before the murder and it had happened around 4:00 in the afternoon when it was still light outside. He contacted police after he saw the same car with the same woman driving it the previous night and had taken down the license plate number. The car was registered to Elam Gray, who was known by the nickname "Butch." The witness said he knew it was the same car because it had a hubcap missing.[79]

Other tips came in, including an anonymous call encouraging police to talk to a Paradise resident and claiming the woman had information about the shooting. Police followed up and the lead went nowhere.[80]

Another tip came in to York County authorities about a man who had told the witness that he had picked up a phone extension in his home and heard his wife talking to Buddy Mills. The anonymous tipster reported that the husband then said he planned to kill Buddy with a shotgun.[81]

A detective from Longview, North Carolina, called in a report from a woman there who claimed her brother-in-law had told her he had committed a murder in Fort Mill.[82] Nothing came of that lead either.

Other suspects and other leads turned up on the radar, including a couple from Hollywood, Florida, two Rock Hill men with rap sheets for burglary and drug offenses, and a reported dark car sitting in the peach trees near the accident site with its lights off and a single occupant who appeared to be smoking a cigarette and watching the scene. Fingers were being pointed in every direction. Even Lynne Gerald's boyfriend's name came up, although his only "crime" seemed to be that he was a twenty-year-old who drove around town in a white Mustang. The leads were going nowhere and no arrests were made.

Besides theories about the jealous revenge of a mistress's husbands and accusations aimed at Shirley and family members, there was also the matter of Buddy's job problems. In his interview with investigators, Terry Gerald had described how Buddy was angry with his former boss at Clairol for closing his territory and laying him off only to reopen the territory and give the job to a new salesman three weeks later. Gerald also mentioned Buddy had been upset in recent days because he had lost out on a promising shot at a new job.[83]

The lack of progress on the case was taking its toll on Buddy's family. In a letter written August 23 to Chief Deputy Gene Ervin, Buddy's sister Lambert Mills described her disappointment that there had been no arrests.

"It was really rough this summer in Fort Mill for us all. Seems like every day something reminded us of Buddy and his unsolved death. I know your dept. is busy with other cases, but I do hope you haven't given up completely on Buddy's—until it is resolved, I think our family will never have peace of mind."

She goes on to talk about cases in the news where psychics are being brought in and even gives a name and number of someone in North Carolina who might be helpful.

"This is just a thought," she wrote. "We'll try anything to solve this."

Lambert didn't live in Fort Mill; she was in North Palm Beach, Florida. But she was concerned for her brother Ladd, who had found Buddy's body.

"Ladd is too nice to 'bug you,' but I wish you would bring him up to date if you can on what's happening. It's easy for him to get depressed over the situation since he is in an area where gossip is constantly reminding him of Buddy."[84]

James Mills, twin brother of Jean and younger brother of Buddy, was an FBI agent based in Los Angeles. He came to Fort Mill for a week each year to visit, and while he was in town he met with York County investigators to check up on the case. He told Bayles and the other family members that there was nothing in the case file that looked as if it would lead to an arrest. The case went cold quickly.

Today Gigi Mills Poole reflects on that time and about the questions that still linger.

"I was such a trusting soul," she says.

Young and overwhelmed by her loss and not wanting to make things more difficult for Shirley, who was grieving the loss as well, Gigi decided she would stand back and let the investigation take its course. At one point, investigators told her their best evidence was actually not admissible in court, and she accepted that they had gone as far as they could. Over the years she has wondered whether or not she should have pushed to keep the case open but ultimately felt the best course of action for her family was to focus on moving forward. Gigi and her father were extremely close and it's unlikely he would have wanted her to spend her life in a consuming quest for justice that might never come. Still her father's daughter, she honors his memory in the way she lives her life rather than by focusing on his death.

Buddy's brother Ladd passed away in 2010. Libba Mills Mack died in 1984, and Evelyn Mills Merritt in 1992. They and their other siblings never got answers to their questions about what happened.

Shirley Mills remarried and passed away in 2007. There is no evidence she or her children had any involvement in Buddy's death. She is buried at Unity Cemetery, not far from Buddy.

Despite all the innuendo and suspicion, all the finger-pointing and accusations, and all the well-meaning suggestions about psychics and surveillance, an arrest was never made. An examination of the police file reveals two documents from 1992 between the SLED Forensic Services Laboratory and the York County Sheriff's office. A letter dated March 16 of that year, nearly ten years after the murder, is a request from Lt. Robert Hudgins of the Criminal Investigative Division of the sheriff's office for "any relative correspondence that you may have or may obtain on this case," and it references the case number for victim Gilbert Mills.[85] After that date, there is nothing more in the file.

The murder of Buddy Mills remains unsolved.

BEHIND
THE BALLOT

---

*When I got out of Davidson, all I knew how to do was run
a political campaign.*

—Bayles Mack

Ever since the time in Bayles's childhood when friend Jimmy Howie
noticed he had an interest in his cousin's campaign, there were
opportunities for Bayles to observe the political process in action
at his father's knee. He had watched his father run in local elections
for town council or the school board and had seen the impact his
influence had. In the 1950s he would have a chance to watch Billee in
action on a friend's campaign for a seat in the United States Senate.

The name Ernest Frederick "Fritz" Hollings is a legendary one in
South Carolina politics. Elected to the state House of Representatives

at twenty-seven, by the time he was thirty-six he was governor. In 1962 he decided to make a run for the United States Senate, challenging incumbent Olin D. Johnston. Billee Mack and Bayles's uncle Cody Smith worked on the campaign and had a close working relationship with Hollings. Bayles observed the inner workings of the campaign and got to know the candidate well. They too would become good friends, with Hollings a frequent guest at Bayles and Joanne's house on Confederate Street playing game after game of tennis on their backyard court. Hollings was unsuccessful in his first run for the Senate, but Johnston passed away during the subsequent term and Hollings came back for a second run against Donald Russell, who had been appointed to the seat until a special election could be held. Ironically, Russell had been Hollings's successor as governor and resigned that office to take the Senate seat. He didn't hold it long. The following year, the special election to determine who would complete the remaining two years of Johnston's term was held, and Hollings defeated Russell in the Democratic primary before going on to defeat the Republican challenger, Marshall Parker, in the general election. He would serve in the Senate for thirty-six years.

By the time Bayles attended the 1972 DNC in Miami, South Carolina had a lieutenant governor Bayles knew well. He had helped him get the job. Earle Morris Jr. was a state senator from Pickens County who had his eyes on sitting in the governor's chair one day. In 1970, candidates for governor and lieutenant governor ran in separate races. They were not a "running mate" ticket. John West was the outgoing lieutenant governor, having served under Bob McNair. He was running for governor this time, and he won the race that fall. Earle Morris's bid for the lieutenant governor's office was successful as well. Bayles had been in charge of raising the money for the Morris campaign, while Don Fowler ran the campaign itself. Bayles knew why they wanted him in charge of bringing in the campaign dollars.

"I was the guy who wasn't afraid to ask for money from all the rich folks."

Though Fowler was the campaign manager, Morris took to addressing Bayles jokingly as "Mr. Chairman," a term he would continue using for years.

Having spent time in both the state House and Senate, Morris knew the ins and outs of how the state ran.

"He knew more about state government than any other person in the world," Bayles recalled, "but he was a naïve politician." He explained what he meant by that comment. "He sort of floated around. He loved to make speeches and he knew everybody. But he didn't have a cause commitment. He wasn't a champion for any cause."

Four years after his win for lieutenant governor, Morris believed he was ready for the top job and announced he would run for governor in 1974. Bayles, Don Fowler, and the state Democratic machine got busy trying to secure a win for him.

Despite his popularity in the state, Morris lost the race in the primary stage. Morris was divorced at a time and in a place where that was a political liability. He also wasn't able to secure the African American votes he needed. His campaign was surprised by how much trouble he was having in that area, especially given Don Fowler's track record.

"If there was anybody who could get black votes, it was Don Fowler, and it just wasn't happening because of the people who were in the race," Bayles affirmed.

Morris's opponents were Charles D. "Pug" Ravenel and William Jennings Bryan Dorn. Ravenel was a member of the venerable Ravenel family of Charleston, but he had been living up North after graduating from prestigious Phillips Exeter Academy in New Hampshire and later from Harvard University. Dorn, named for the famous orator William Jennings Bryan, was a World War II veteran who had served in the state House and Senate before he was elected to the US House of Representatives in 1946. He had run unsuccessfully for the Senate in 1948 and continued serving in the House.

Seven names appeared as gubernatorial candidates on the ballot for the Democratic primary in July. Earle Morris placed third, ending his hopes for the office. Ravenel and Dorn were the top two finishers respectively, with the results so close it triggered a run-off election. Ravenel prevailed once again in the run-off, but his viability was under challenge because state law required five years of prior residency for candidates. Ultimately, the South Carolina Supreme Court found he did not meet the requirement, and a special convention was held in which Dorn was selected to be the Democratic candidate.

The Morris loss set up what Bayles remembered as his worst run of luck with any campaign for office. Fowler, Bayles, and other members of the state Democratic Executive Committee needed to get behind the Democratic candidate for the general election, whoever that turned out to be. With Morris defeated, they turned their attention to working on behalf of Pug Ravenel. When Ravenel was denied the candidacy by the Supreme Court, Bayles and the others had to focus on getting Dorn elected. He would face Republican candidate James B. Edwards in the general election.

South Carolina had not had a Republican governor since David Henry Chamberlain was elected one hundred years earlier. Prior to 1926, governors in the state served two-year terms, which meant Chamberlain was running for a second term in 1876. This time he faced off against the Democratic nominee, Wade Hampton III. Hampton, of the eponymous Confederate Army unit "Hampton's Legion," came from a family of wealthy and politically-connected Charleston planters and soldiers. His father, Wade Hampton II, had been a dragoon officer in the War of 1812 and served under Andrew Jackson at the famous Battle of New Orleans. His grandfather, the first Wade Hampton, had served in the Revolutionary War. As the namesake of both men, Hampton had a heavy mantle to wear—a legacy of achievement in war, commerce, and politics.

After the Civil War, Republicans, the party of Lincoln and therefore the victors, had swept into office riding the wave of Reconstruction. But Reconstruction itself proved to be unpopular with whites and African Americans alike. Promises made to newly-freed slaves went unmet, and racial discrimination was on the rise. White citizens were unhappy with what they saw as the punitive nature of Reconstruction. They resented the occupying presence of Union soldiers, the influx of carpetbaggers, and the economic and physical destruction the war had caused. Their way of life had ended and they needed to blame someone. By the 1876 election, anti-Republican sentiment in the state had grown more virulent, and the stage was set for what would be the closest gubernatorial race South Carolina had ever seen.

Democrat Wade Hampton won the popular vote by only 1,134 votes, a margin of 50.3 percent to incumbent Chamberlain's 49.1 percent. Republicans were not ready to concede, believing the Hampton victory had come by means of the Democrats suppressing African American votes through bribery and intimidation. The dispute continued, with each side claiming victory. Hampton began setting up a side government, while Chamberlain continued with his established one. Eventually Chamberlain secured federal troops and deployed them around the state capitol in an attempt to maintain his hold on power. Both men appealed to newly inaugurated President Rutherford B. Hayes for recognition as the legitimate governor of the state and federal support to enforce such if needed. Hayes, who was himself a Republican, ordered the troops to stand down. Having a Republican president decline to support his claim, Chamberlain knew his fight was over. He finally conceded the election and went so far as to leave the state.

Ninety-eight years later, the election numbers would be closer than they had been since that contentious race in the wake of the Civil War. Republican James Edwards garnered an identical percentage to that of Wade Hampton—50.3 percent. But this time there was more of a gap between first and second place. Dorn's run for the office ended with 47.0 percent of the vote. Fortunately, this time the office changed party hands without a protracted battle or troops stationed around the capitol.

For Bayles, the period from the Democratic primary in July until the general election in November had been a whirlwind, with his efforts called upon in support of three separate candidates. In the end, none were successful. He remembered the election philosophically.

"I lost three times in that governor's race. That's hard to do."

In 1976 Earle Morris would run and win the job as the state's Comptroller General, a position he occupied until 1999. His 1972 gubernatorial campaign had ended in substantial debt, which friends and supporters worked for years to retire. As a private businessman, he ran afoul of the law and was convicted of securities fraud. He was sentenced to four years in prison but gained early release due to cancer. He died in 2011.

Bayles's involvement in political campaigns most often took the form of fundraising. When John West ran for governor the same year that Earle Morris was elected lieutenant governor, Bayles was asked by a bank officer to sign a promissory note for a loan of $25,000 for street money to get people to the polls on election day. He wanted to know who else was being asked to co-sign for the loan and was told the bank was considering asking Anne Springs Close to do so. The Close family was active in Democratic politics. Bayles, Anne Springs Close, and three others ultimately cosigned the loan and John West's campaign borrowed the money. The bank executive told Bayles that Ms. Close had made a comment about Bayles when she was asked about signing.

"I don't know if it's true," Bayles remembered, "but he told me she said, 'If Bayles signs it, I'll sign it—because I know he'll work some way to get it paid without us having to pay it.'"

"I never did ask her if that story was true," he reminisced.

Governor John West gave Bayles his first state appointment when he took office. West appointed him to a committee that also included two members of the House and two of the Senate with the mandate to re-codify the state's criminal laws. Prior to that time, all state laws of any type were spread out over forty volumes. Criminal statues might be sprinkled in with laws about health department violations or child custody. The committee spent one year pulling together all the criminal statues into two volumes. The updated code was published around 1976.

While Bayles would restrict his own involvement in public office to time spent as chairman of the York County Council, an office to which he was elected in 1976, he would devote much of his time and energy to being a force behind those whose names appeared on ballots. His father had been the Democratic Executive Committeeman for Fort Mill precinct #1 and Bayles was elected as his successor in

1974, making him the "big cheese" in his near-exclusive Democratic precinct. His role there was to get the word out about the candidates, secure the poll workers, make sure people showed up to vote, and oversee the certification of the ballot counts. Two callers would call out the votes while two tabulators recorded them and added them up. Bayles would turn in the official results. Fort Mill #1 was the largest precinct in York County for years, so having an influence on the ballot box was no small thing in the area's political landscape. He said he could almost always predict how the vote would come out by who showed up to vote.

"Don't worry about the count—you're going to win. I see who's coming in here and I know how they're going to vote," he once told a candidate who was worried about his chances on election day.

Knowing and being able to predict the actions of the electorate was a skill he would hone at the district and state level. Besides watching his father do the job, he was also leaning on what he had learned in his undergraduate studies.

"When I got out of Davidson, all I knew how to do was run a political campaign." He had been active in student government and was part of the inter-fraternity council as well as president of his own fraternity during his time there. Some of his classmates pressured him to run for student body president. Instead, he talked a friend into running and backed him. His decision not to run, but rather to help behind the scenes, was a prescient indicator of things to come.

In 1982 Bayles received a phone call from his friend John Spratt Jr. The son of the banker and attorney whom Bayles had spent his summers working for, and his predecessor as town attorney, John Spratt Sr., the younger Spratt was considering a run for the US House for the seat currently occupied by Bayles's fellow 1968

Chicago DNC delegate, Ken Holland. Holland had won the seat in 1974 after Bayles's former employer, Congressman Tom Gettys, declined to run for a sixth term. It was the same seat his coalition of South Carolina young political operatives had suggested he run for that he ultimately declined because his family did not want to return to Washington.

With the seat coming open again, Spratt thought Bayles might want to make a play for it, so he called to test the waters. Lightly treading into the subject as gentlemen politicians are wont to do, Spratt told Bayles he might be interested in running, but only if Bayles wasn't already planning to. When Bayles told him he wasn't planning a run, Spratt took the opportunity to grab him for another role, asking Bayles to run his campaign. In a single phone call, Spratt neutralized a potential rival and locked up a campaign operative all at once. It proved to be a successful partnership. Spratt won the seat, and held it for twenty-eight years. While in office he was a fierce advocate for children's health and a balanced budget.

After spending his life as a Democrat, Bayles found the winds of political change threatening to sweep him out of the party in the early 2000s. He wasn't interested in going willingly.

"I was a Democrat because it was inclusive. The Republicans were exclusive. I was a fiscal conservative but a Democrat in every other way."

However, the tenor of the nation was changing. Bayles blamed Republican gerrymandering and other changes in the traditional role of the parties for creating a disconnect between what the Democratic Party had once been and what it was becoming. He described attending his first Republican meetings and finding they were "less fun than any political meeting I'd been to. They were stodgy," he remembered.

He also had an opinion about what kind of people tended to be members of the GOP.

"You had to be high-falutin' in order to be a Republican and I never felt like I was high-falutin'. I certainly wasn't in my politics."

But change was coming, whether he liked it or not. Many of his friends were abandoning the Democrats and turning up in Republican circles. Eventually he found himself doing the same, with a great deal of regret.

"I wasn't deserting my friends. I was just deserting the party. The party was causing all the problems."

In later years Bayles's activity in political campaigns was mostly limited to supporting them financially. He never again served on the executive team of any campaign or took to the state's highways to shake hands and solicit voter support. He was ready to settle down to more of an observer role and thought back to the years he had spent both behind the scenes and in various elected or appointed positions.

"There seems to be no compassion, not only in government but also in politics today. They can't get as much accomplished as we used to, and the reason is that we have no leadership in politics today and there's no courage," he lamented.

Despite his success in the world of politics, he takes a dim view of its future.

"I always thought it was an honorable profession, and I was involved in it for fifty years. I'd be ashamed to be doing it today."

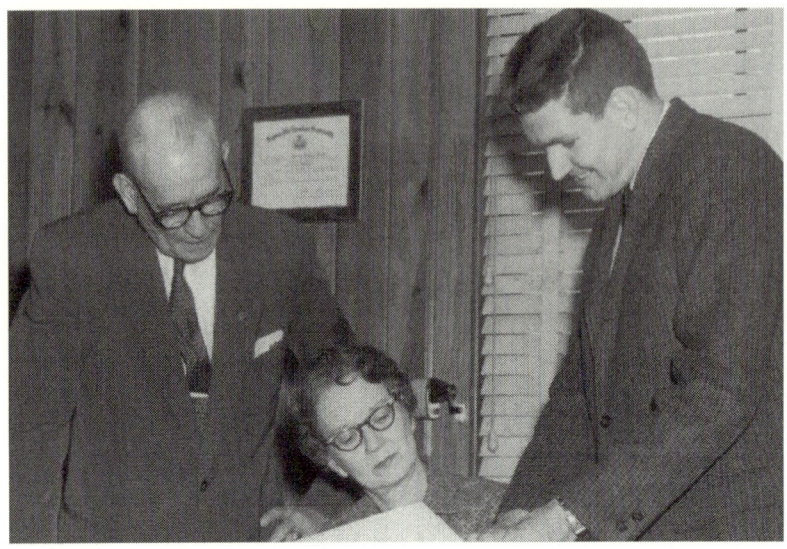

J.C. Godfrey, Evelyn Mills Merritt, and Bayles in the office of the Fort Mill Credit Bureau in March 1961. The company was one of Bayles's first forays into sideline businesses in addition to his law career.

Official pass for the 1968 Democratic National Convention in Chicago.

Bayles upon election as Chairman of the York County Council, 1976.

Buddy Mills in the early 1980s.

Bayles business portrait circa late 1980s.

Transportation representatives at the site of one of two bridges to be torn down to make way for the new Arthur Ravenel Jr. Bridge linking Mount Pleasant, South Carolina to Charleston, South Carolina. L to R: Marvin Stevenson, Bob Harrell, Bayles Mack, Buck Limehouse, Tee Hopper, Bobby Jones, and Moot Truluck.

Department of Transportation (formerly Highway Commission) commissioners in the early 1990s. L to R: Howell Clyburn, Morgan Martin, Gene Stoddard, John Hardy, Ron Joye (Assistant to DOT), Bob Harrell, Bayles Mack, and Moot Truluck.

Bayles as highway commissioner making a presentation in one of the counties in his district.

Bayles at the dedication of the South Carolina welcome center's monument recognizing the naming of the B. Bayles Mack Highway.

Bayles (far right) and representatives of the Department of Transportation at the dedication of a monument memorializing the naming of the B. Bayles Mack Highway. The monument stands at the South Carolina welcome center.

Northbound I-77 near Highway 9 in Chester County. The state named the section of interstate from this point to the North Carolina/South Carolina state line in honor of Bayles for his years of dedicated service to the Highway Commission (later Department of Transportation). One of his major accomplishments while on the commission included championing the construction of the stretch of interstate that joins Charlotte, North Carolina and Columbia, South Carolina.

Bayles participating in a living history video project for the Fort Mill History Museum, 2016. The interview was recorded in the library of the Springs family's White Homestead.

The Elizabeth Mills Mack train car that Bayles restored and uses as one of his offices. The Fort Mill sign is from the original depot from the days when the town had daily passenger and freight service.

Bayles with grandson William Reigel in the train car office, 2022.

Bayles in his lovingly restored train car office, 2022.

IN THE SERVICE OF THE STATE

*South Carolina is too small for a republic and too large for
an insane asylum.*

—James L. Petigru

Billee Mack had told his son early in his career not to run for office at
the town council or school board level because his neighbors would
constantly be bombarding him with local issues and he would never
have any peace. He had told him to run at the county level if he ran
at all, and Bayles had done that. During his second term as chairman
of the York County Council in the late 1970s, he had an opportunity
to put more of his father's advice into practice. The local Democratic
delegation came to him with an idea—they wanted him to run for the
state's highway commission. The Department of Transportation was

the largest of all the state departments and had the biggest budget, larger than health and environmental control, more than prisons, more than ETV. It was the place where a commissioner could have the most impact and best serve the citizens of South Carolina. Running for this board where commissioners are elected by the state legislature would mean resigning his county council seat, so he asked his father for advice.

"If they want you to go on the highway commission, you do it, because it's the biggest agency. There's more money in the highway department than in any other state agency. You follow the money. DOT is where you can serve more citizens than any other place in the state," Billee told him.

Bayles agreed it would be a good opportunity and one where he could have an impact because he already knew so much about the landscape of the state and its people. He turned in his resignation to the county council and set about getting himself elected to the commission. It was 1979, and at that time commission representation was divided up by judicial circuits resulting in sixteen members who elected their chairman from among that number. Bayles's friend Billy Hayes held the local seat and had let him know he wasn't going to stand for consideration again. His opponent for the seat would be Sam Fewell, a former state legislator in the House. Fewell had resigned his legislative seat, and Bayles's law partner Palmer Freeman had secured it.

Bayles was elected by the legislature to serve his judicial district, which included York and Union counties, and was sworn in the day of the election by John Campbell, the former mayor of Columbia and by that time secretary of state, in his office. Commission policy called for terms of four years each with a restriction against serving back-to-back terms. With the requisite one-term-on, one-term-off rotation, Bayles would serve a total of sixteen years between 1979 and 2004. To this day he is the longest-serving commissioner with four terms.

Bayles's longstanding practice of getting to know as many people as he could all over the state worked in his favor after he won his seat when a friend from Columbia spoke on his behalf to Dr. Bill Berne, then chairman of the highway commission who was in charge of committee assignments. The friend encouraged Berne to "give Bayles whatever committee he wants."

"He didn't even know me," Bayles recalls, "but he asked me if I had a preference and I told him I want to be where the money is and the money is in construction and maintenance."

Dr. Berne was surprised by the request, telling Bayles that most people wanted to be on the committee that dealt with the highway patrol for which the commission had oversight. Bayles had specific reasons for his wish to serve on the construction and maintenance committee instead.

"Ninety-three percent of the money in DOT was in that committee. I had the best job I could get. Everybody wanted the patrols because that was glamorous. Everybody wanted to not have to get a ticket. I was after construction and maintenance because you were serving the people when you had that. I set the agenda for every road to be paved for four years. And every road I wanted I had in there."

Dr. Berne gave him what he wanted and then some. At the first meeting the name "Bayles Mack" not only appeared under the heading for the construction and maintenance committee, but he was also listed as its chairman. Down the road he would rise to become chairman of the full highway commission.

All the talk of following the money wasn't about personal power for Bayles. It was a practical reality that helping get projects done required the funding to do them. Government agencies are notoriously underfunded, and competition for available dollars is fierce. Whether a public servant is elected *to the legislature* by the people or *by the legislature* (whom the people have previously elected), the mandate is the same—get results for the constituents of your district. Serving the state's largest agency on that agency's best-funded committee allowed Bayles to do a lot for his district and the state.

Official highway commission meeting minutes show Bayles was officially seated on April 9, 1979. During his first term he learned a great deal about infrastructure needs across the state and helped spearhead projects through the system and pave roads from the coast to the upstate.

One major project was preparing to celebrate a milestone during Bayles's first term. Interstate 77, the north-south route that traverses South Carolina from the upper part of the state at the North Carolina line below Charlotte to Columbia, was ready to mark its completion in December 1981. The expansion of the interstate that began in 1970 for those seventy-five miles ultimately cost the state $171 million. The northernmost section, which cuts through Fort Mill, was completed in 1975. As it made its way south of town, the road passed right by CBI Inc.'s Ramada Inn at Rock Hill, with an exchange ramp right at its front door, just as Bayles and his hotel partners had predicted years earlier. He and fellow commissioner F. S. McWhirter presided over the ribbon-cutting ceremony that featured Gov. Richard Riley as keynote speaker to officially open the final 21.4-mile section.

By the time his second commission term began in April 1987, there had been a change in the makeup of the commission's membership. In addition to the sixteen judicial district representatives, there were now four members from the state legislature: two from the House and two from the Senate. The group also grew by one direct appointment by the governor. It was not the most popular action. In fact, the commissioners had an unwritten rule that the governor's appointee would not be elected chairman. It was their way of ensuring the state's chief executive couldn't wield undue influence. They would continue to elect their chairman from the district members, and in the second half of his term Bayles found himself the new holder of that title. It was a role among peers, but it wasn't without influence.

"It's more honorary, but if you use it right, it's a big deal," Bayles recalled.

The commission's quiet act of rebellion about electing its chairman would not survive future structural changes by the legislature.

When Bayles began his third term in 1995, even more changes in the makeup of the commission had taken effect. Bayles wasn't enthusiastic about the changes.

"The legislature in their wisdom reconstructed the whole commission and cut it to six people with a chairman appointed by the governor. I never wanted to be a gubernatorial appointee, I can tell you, because you answered to one person only and nobody respected you. If you were legislative you had more clout."

Instead of representing judicial districts, the legislature had decided the commissioners would represent congressional districts instead. That meant more counties would be covered by each commissioner. In another change to the board's structure, a seventh member would be added by gubernatorial appointment. Under the new rules, the governor's appointee would be the commission's chairman.

At the beginning of his third term, Bayles was elected vice-chairman by his fellow commissioners. As they waited for the governor's appointee to be named and take his place as chairman of the board, work wasn't getting done. The delay in the appointee's approval by the legislature was taking too long.

Bayles suggested the commission needed to start meeting and keep things moving. At least one member of the board responded that they couldn't meet without a chairman.

Bayles disagreed and asked, "Are you going to let the people of the state suffer until you get one?"

The governor's appointee was not approved by the legislature for eight months, during which time the commission did not let the people of the state suffer. They held their meetings with Bayles serving as de-facto chair in the interim.

By the time Bayles began his fourth term in 2000, South Carolina was under the leadership of a new governor, Jim Hodges. One of Hodges's priorities involved a shift in policy orientation for the highway commission. The edict came down that the state commission needed to work on improving relationships with federal representatives to help bring more federal road dollars to the state. To that end, the commission hired a Washington, D.C., attorney and lobbyist with strong ties to South Carolina. John Napier, originally of Bennettsville, had represented the sixth congressional district in the US House of Representatives in the 1980s and was later appointed to the Court of Federal Claims bench by President Ronald Reagan. By the late 1990s Napier was practicing law and working as a lobbyist in the nation's capital. The South Carolina Department of Transportation was a new client for him, and he worked extensively with Bayles on the initiative requested by the governor. He had known Bayles prior, but it was during this time that their relationship really took off.

Napier recalls the special talent Bayles brought to large and complicated transportation projects. "You can't say that big projects like that come together at any one point. That's why Bayles with his [experience in] transportation, industrial, and economic development for the State of South Carolina was so important because his career transcends a lot of that. He has a little bit here, a little bit there, and a little bit here in his influences that he represented. Some were not even when he was on the commission, but derived from his time as a private practitioner because he represented so many interests and they would go to him as a go-to man, particularly in the development of the mid part of South Carolina. If I had a problem in York County or anywhere in South Carolina where there was economic development or transportation policy or in many other situations, I wouldn't hesitate to pick up the phone and say to a client, 'We need to associate Bayles Mack on this thing because he's got these qualities that will help solve the problem.'"

When Bayles began his fourth term he was eager to resume working with DOT's top executive. Elizabeth Mabry had been legal counsel for the department for fourteen years before she became its executive director, the same position that is called secretary of transportation today, during Bayles's third term in 1996. Having worked with Bayles in this earlier term and then again in his fourth and final term, she has a unique perspective on his role with the commission. She described a groundbreaking DOT program Bayles had been instrumental in setting up. Called "27-in-7," it was a large, comprehensive bond program, the first of such scale the state DOT had ever embarked on.

Mabry described the way it was designed to work. "In the program, what we did was take what would have taken us twenty-seven years to accomplish under standard DOT practices, which is pay-as-you-go. I'll explain it like this: say you're going to build a house but you don't borrow money and each year you do a little bit and a little bit and a little bit, but under the '27-in-7' we issued highway bonds and did all twenty-seven years' worth of work in seven years. It was a very significant program. We had over $3 billion dollars of work going on during that time.

"The projects were selected by the various councils of government. The COGs and the metropolitan planning organizations met with our engineers and they came up with the projects that were most important for those areas. For relieving congestion, for widening, for economic development, whatever reasons that they were significant, these groups would put them in order of significance, and then that's how we would build them using the money that was allocated to that specific district. There were all kinds of different projects."

The program's success garnered attention across the country, bringing representatives from Washington, Arizona, and other states to Columbia to find out how the South Carolina program had been structured. It even got international recognition and resulted in a Russian delegation making the journey as well.

Mabry remembers Bayles's involvement in bringing it to fruition. "Bayles was instrumental because he was an attorney, and it takes a lot of legal technicalities and legal procedures to go through to start a large bonding program. So he was very, very valuable to me in combing through the legal mechanisms we had to go through, which were quite complicated."

During Bayles's fourth term, some of the state's projects more recognizable in recent years were beginning to take shape. One in particular would change the skyline of the state's largest city.

If you happened to be a visitor in Charleston prior to 2005 and you wanted to cross the Cooper River to Mount Pleasant and then come back into the city, you were in for a harrowing experience. The old bridges could leave the most confident drivers white-knuckled and praying to their higher power that they wouldn't end up in the drink.

The John P. Grace Memorial Bridge, opened in 1929, was the only means of crossing by automobile for thirty-seven years. Today the ubiquitous ghost tours in the city tell visitors stories about a worker on the bridge falling into one of the concrete pillars as they were being poured, forever entombing him inside. Or the story of a family whose car plunged off the bridge and into the river and the legend that you can see the car with the family inside on the bridge on a foggy night. If any of these visitors ever traveled on this bridge, or its companion, the Silas N. Pearman Bridge, built in 1966, the horror stories might seem eminently plausible. Six years before construction began on a modern bridge to replace it, the Grace Memorial Bridge scored only four points out of one hundred on an industry safety scale. As bad as that was, by comparison it felt less treacherous to drive across than the Pearman. The Pearman Bridge was added to alleviate congested traffic, leaving the Grace to carry vehicles out of Charleston and the Pearman to bring them back in. However, poor ratings on the Grace resulted in it being closed to large or heavy trucks. That meant the Pearman would have to do double duty and one of its two lanes was reversed so traffic on it went in both directions. Though newer and in better mechanical shape than the Grace, the Pearman was not for the faint of heart. With barely any space between vehicles and the outer guardrail and no rail separating the oncoming lanes, it was the site of several fatal head-on crashes. Eventually plastic lane dividers were added between the oncoming lanes, but that did nothing about the lack of space between vehicles and the inadequate-looking rail that kept them from plunging off the side and down two hundred fifty feet to the water below. Drivers were faced with the nerve-racking task of trying to avoid cars coming at them while not hitting the rail and tumbling over the edge.

Finally plans were made to replace both spans with one that would meet the needs of commuters as well as pedestrians for years to come. Funding it was on the agenda during Bayles's fourth term.

The proposed Arthur Ravenel Jr. Bridge, beautifully designed and not at all harrowing to traverse, came before the commission with a price tag of $680 million. The seven members of the commission were split on whether or not to approve the expenditure. The final vote was four to three in favor of funding it. Bayles was the swing vote and used the opportunity to gain something for the people back in his home district. The highway commission was, after all, the group that worked out all the politics surrounding highway projects.

York County had just adopted a new program to raise money to help fund road projects outside of money offered by the state. Called "Pennies for Progress," the program would add one cent to sales tax within the county over a seven-year period. All the money would be earmarked specifically for road projects. The projected income was $99 million. Bayles saw an opportunity to negotiate for additional funding to "match" the "Pennies for Progress" funds and the state actually came through with $165 million.

The State Infrastructure Bank, called the SIB, is a separate organization responsible for allocation of federal funds for interstate work. Aside from the money that came to it at that time from the federal government, the state was also kicking in funding to the SIB because state law had not been changed to collect an adequate amount of gas taxes. The state set aside $50 million for the SIB for maintenance work on the section of I-77 that had been completed during Bayles's first term on the commission. This included interstate running through York County. An additional $35–$40 million was allocated to repave the York County section of I-77 with an impervious surface to prevent hydroplaning.

The other major projects that got their start during Bayles's fourth term were the Greenville Bypass Toll Road, the Bobby Jones Freeway in North Augusta and Aiken, Veterans Highway in Horry County, and Carolina Bays Parkway in Horry County.

Looking back, Bayles opined on his time with the commission.

"What I was good at, and I may not be good at anything else, but what I was good at was knowing where there were pots of money and I knew where every pot was and I knew how much was in every pot. I would access each one of them in a way that would help us gather all the money up to spend in York County. If not York County, then in my district. If not in my district, then on special projects like the Charleston bridge."

Charleston got its bridge and York County got quite a lot of money for its infrastructure. "Pennies for Progress" was so successful that the program has been renewed three times since it originated. It continues to provide significant funding for road projects in the fast-growing county.

When asked if he was ever offered bribes or approached by anyone to use his influence inappropriately, Bayles had an emphatic answer.

"In the whole time I was in politics, nobody ever offered me money. I don't know if they thought I wouldn't take it or that I would turn them in. I did everything above board. I just worked the commission for my project benefit. The way I felt about it was that it was a way I could serve the whole state."

He felt strongly enough about his service that he wasn't bothered by the idea of anyone questioning the people he worked with about it.

"Go down there and ask some of that crowd and they'll tell you I worked harder at it than anybody else, and the reason I did, I knew that I had to in order to really accomplish something. And the rest of them didn't give a damn. They didn't care. They were interested in tickets being fixed and stuff like that," he remembered.

Elizabeth Mabry concurred, recalling Bayles's positive attitude and willingness to seek compromise for the benefit of the all involved.

"Bayles Mack was a gentleman. He really and truly was a gentleman. He came onto the commission and was very supportive of all of the employees, which makes a big difference because work does not get done without the people out on the highways and the engineers in the office. He supported the employees and was concerned about the employees. That was very significant to me because not all commissioners are. Bayles was extraordinarily supportive of the everyday person and also of the leadership. He was supportive of me. I always could count on Bayles to ask the questions and understand what was going on and then support the idea and even enhance the idea if he could. That support meant a lot. It made things run smoothly," Mabry recalled.

She continued, "He also was so cheerful. That big smile was always there. He had fun. 'He puts the *fun* in funding,' we'd always say. He was happy, he was cheerful, and he was a peacemaker. Because if you get seven or eight people together in a room, there are going to be some disagreements from time to time about how things should be done or just personality issues. Bayles was always the peacemaker. He would make sure that the issue was resolved and he wanted everyone to be satisfied. And that made a big difference, to have someone who sought the common ground and looked for a peaceful and happy resolution. He wanted everybody to have fun doing their work. He's a remarkable man."

John Napier concurred on Bayles's ability to seek a win-win solution for all involved. "It's like that old saying by Winston Churchill. Someone asked Churchill what a diplomat was, and he replied, 'A diplomat is the sort of fellow who can tell you to go to hell and you ask him how to get there.' And that's the way Bayles is. His conversations with you, whatever he is doing, he always turns it into a positive, pleasant thing. That's an uncommon trait. If we had more of that, we'd be a whole lot better off."

Friends Johnny Neal and Harry Hogue worked for Bayles during his time on the commission and recall his eagerness to help his home district whenever possible. Hogue talked about the time that $19 million dollars had been allocated for Clover for a proposed bypass. However, the people of Clover were very vocal about not wanting the bypass to be built, so Bayles reassigned the money to Lancaster County.

"Now they [Clover] wish they had done it because traffic is horrendous. Lancaster was very appreciative to get it," Hogue explained. "He secured a lot of money for the areas he was over."

Part of Johnny Neal's job was delivering the checks all over the state. "Most of the people on the commission were just there to bump along their own districts, but Bayles was trying to help everybody."

Harry Hogue remembered one resident in Clover who was upset because the highway commission had taken a small strip of her land for road use and had not paid her anything for it. "To her it was a humongous piece of land—you know what I mean," Hogue said.

She reached out to Bayles and he told her he would see what he could do. Legislators each had an allotment of "C-funds," limited amounts of money at their disposal that could be used for small projects at their discretion.

Hogue reported the results of Bayles's inquiry: "By him looking into it, they came back and paid that lady $5,000 for that strip of land they had taken. That made Bayles a big man in her eyes. She was very appreciative and always talked highly of Bayles."

He definitely did a tremendous amount of good for his district and for the state during his time on the commission, but at least on one occasion he wasn't above letting his position work in his favor. Once again, it was Harry Hogue who was there to bear witness. It was something that happened on their drive to Myrtle Beach one day.

"I can tell you a funny story on that. He and I were going to the beach, and when we got to Florence we had run over one of those ropes that the highway puts out to notify them of your speed. About a mile down the road they had a whole unit sitting there to stop you and ask you all the questions and everything."

Harry described the scene: "Sure enough, when we pulled up, the officer came over and Bayles handed him his license and registration and he said, 'Officer, how're you doing?'"

The officer said, "Fine."

"Here's my registration and license, and while you're checking them, would you mind checking my tag? It's rattling a little bit back there.'"

The tag was an official highway commission plate that also indicated he was the chairman of said commission. Back then the commission had total control over the patrol division. The officer stepped back to the driver's door and handed back the license and registration before telling him, "Mr. Mack, everything is in order and your tag is very secure."

"And down the road we went," Hogue recalled with a laugh. "It was quick thinking on his part!"

Despite the actions of that particular day, Bayles had a reputation within the commission for frowning on anyone using their position to try fixing tickets in order to curry favor in their districts. On that subject, one particular commissioner came to mind during Bayles's time as chairman.

"I had a commissioner from the upstate come to me, and he would always walk around with a cigarette in his mouth; when he talked to you there would be ashes on the end of it."

He approached Bayles one day, ash-laden cigarette in place, and the conversation turned to promises this commissioner had made to people in his district. The Greenville man began by telling Bayles "they" had told him Bayles was the man to see to get things done. When responding to the question of who "they" were, the purpose of the conversation was finally revealed.

"My boys here at the commission," the commissioner responded. "I've got some tickets and I promised my friends I'd get them taken care of."

"You can't do that," Bayles told the man. "They'll put you in jail, my friend. You can't do that." Bayles's knowledge of the law and his having served as a magistrate in 1969 and 1970 meant that he had a firm grasp of the do's and don'ts.

Referring to the fact that the commission had oversight of the highway patrol, the man pressed on. "We run the patrol. How come I can't?"

"You just can't," Bayles responded. He then offered to at least take a look at them to see if he could help some other way.

"I was a magistrate one time and I learned a lot about that," Bayles explained. "I told him, 'You just give them to me and I'll talk to the magistrate and the magistrate will talk to the patrolman and maybe they will reduce them. Maybe they'll get a two-point instead of a four-point.'"

It turned out the commissioner had brought them with him and when he retrieved them from his car, Bayles was surprised to see him holding more than forty citations. He knew any help he could offer would take a great deal of time because each one would have to be examined and addressed individually with a magistrate. He took the citations and cautioned the man.

"You leave these alone. Don't you do what you said you were thinking about doing because if you went to the patrolman and told him he's got to fix it and you're running the patrol, they're going to put you in jail."

"Aww, they ain't going to do that, are they?" The commissioner refused to believe there was any problem with what he wanted to do.

Bayles looked at the citations and talked to the magistrate about any that were minor enough to be eligible for reduction and any others for which there might be some consideration for leniency. The magistrate took it from there and they were able to get some helpful form of resolution on all of them. Bayles returned the citations to the commissioner with the instructions written on each for what the drivers needed to do, such as paying fines, to close their cases. Again, he warned the commissioner not to involve himself in these actions in the future and tried to talk to him about the broader purpose of serving on the commission. The man was unimpressed.

"All I care about is having that numbered tag so they won't stop me," the man said, referring to the special state license plates commissioners were assigned during their terms.

"Why would anybody take a job for that?" Bayles wondered years later. "They wanted the honor and they wanted the tag. I knew if I paid more attention than they did, I would get whatever I wanted," he recalled, referring to his project agenda.

Another incident stood out from his four terms and this one referred to a fellow commissioner's submission of a "cuff" item. Projects that were not on the main list could be added "off the cuff" for consideration and usually involved small paving projects or other relatively minor requests from the various districts. A new commissioner mentioned there was a dirt road he would like to see paved but wasn't sure how to get it done. Bayles told him to submit it as a cuff item. The man did, and during a break in the meeting the engineers who were in attendance came as a group to speak to Bayles privately. They told him the commissioner should not be submitting the road as a paving project.

"Why not? It's in his district, isn't it?" Bayles asked.

"Yes. But it runs through his farm," came the response.

Bayles spoke to the commissioner and told him it was inappropriate and that he would have to make a motion that it be removed from the list but that it would look better if the commissioner made the motion himself. He told the commissioner the appropriate action would be to request the engineers take a look at the dirt road and see if they believed it qualified for surfacing. If so, then the engineers could propose adding it to the list.

When the meeting reconvened, the commissioner explained that he had thought better of the request and that he would like to request it be removed from the list so state engineers could evaluate it. It was an almost word-for-word parroting of Bayles's explanation to him. However, another commissioner caught on that the man had been trying to get a road on his own property paved and called him out on it, telling him he hadn't had a right to propose it in the first place. The commissioner's response still made Bayles shake his head in disbelief decades later.

The man had responded incredulously to the whole group, saying, "How come I couldn't? I paid $65,000 to get this job!"

"He was a nice guy, but he was oblivious to government and to legal life," Bayles observed.

＊

Beyond interstates and state highways, transportation in the region was also of interest to Bayles. He served on the Metropolitan Transit Committee and they were considering a new project. Amtrak had a line running from Raleigh to Charlotte and on to Greenville and there was interest in adding service from Charlotte to Columbia, which would connect the North and South Carolina capitals. Senators Fritz Hollings and Strom Thurmond were supportive of the initiative, and Hollings served on the Senate Appropriations Committee, which had Amtrak as part of its purview. A deal was struck to obtain funding of $2 million from SCDOT to operate a year-long test of the route. The Feds would lease the cars from North Carolina and pay railway company Norfolk & Southern for use of the rails. After one year, if the service proved to be commercially viable, the federal government would take over operating costs. Bayles, Amtrak executives, and elected officials from cities along the proposed route embarked on a symbolic train journey from Charlotte to Columbia as part of a demonstration and photo op, and the deal was officially signed while en route. With all indicators looking positive, word came down from Washington that the Amtrak budget was to be cut that year. The Charlotte-to-Columbia line was no longer an option, and the deal never got beyond that demo run. Still, it was a forward-thinking initiative for a region that by the 2010s would be growing at a rate that outpaced a good portion of the nation.

＊

Back in 1984, three years after the completion of the I-77 extension, a concurrent resolution by the state House and Senate was passed naming the section of I-77 from the North Carolina line to the intersection with South Carolina Highway No. 9 the "B. Bayles Mack Highway." At the time Bayles was hesitant to accept the honor, fearing it would give the appearance that his work with the commission was self-serving. He had to be talked into consenting to have the resolution submitted for affirmation by the Department of Transportation. The final step in formally naming the section in his honor was affirmed September 20, 2001. Signs went up beside the interstate and a ceremony followed at the Springs Dairy Barn in Fort Mill. Getting his consent had taken seventeen years—more than enough time to quell any accusations of personal glory-seeking.

*

If you live in a city in the Southeast, especially one that's growing at a rapid pace, invariably someone will look you in the eye one day and say something about how terrible it would be for your city to become "another Atlanta." The endless gridlock causing commuters to spend hours of their week bumper-to-bumper with strangers instead of at home with family makes the city a cautionary tale for places like Charlotte.

The concept of managed growth has been on the minds of planners and economic developers for decades. Bayles spent years serving on various boards dedicated to those issues. In addition to his work with the York County Economic Development Board and the Fort Mill Economic Council, he worked on a larger scale with regional partnerships that consider the metropolitan area around Charlotte. One of those was the Charlotte Regional Partnership. It began as part of the Charlotte Chamber of Commerce and was started by some of the city's most influential business leaders. Hugh McCall of Bank of America, Ed Crutchfield from First Union, Bill Lee of Duke Energy, John Belk of the Belk retail chain, Stuart Dickson of the Ruddick Corporation, and others had a vision for strengthening the economic vitality of the region and managing its growth in a way that would enable to it thrive without succumbing to some of the pitfalls of beleaguered Atlanta. Bayles was part of the group, the only South Carolinian on the board, and he would become the organization's chairman in 1995.

South Carolina had not always factored into economic planning in Charlotte, but simple geography dictated that a robust and growing city would not be able to contain everything it hoped to bring to the area without eventually crossing the border. Once the idea took hold, the group evolved to become the Carolinas Partnership and cut ties with the chamber to form a separate organizational body. Eventually the group rebranded itself as Charlotte USA, and its efforts have been instrumental in turning the region into the economic powerhouse it is today. And the benefits are not limited strictly to the immediate vicinity. Charlotte USA made the initial contacts that would ultimately land BMW in the town of Greer, South Carolina.

Bayles served as the organization's chairman for two years. Still, he never considered himself to be in the same league with the major power players.

"They were big boys. I was a small guy. But I had the opportunity to learn from them and be in their company and be a part of organizing the regional partnership."

He credits Duke Energy's Bill Lee with mentoring him and teaching him an important lesson about sustainable economic development. Bill Lee was the education guy, Bayles remembered.

"He told me if you don't have an educated workforce you're not going to have good business. The business is not going to come. When he said educated he meant skilled too. He could see the world changing," Bayles said, reiterating how valuable and accurate Lee's vision turned out to be.

As a result of his work with Charlotte USA and the reputation he had built in the region, Bayles got a call one day from the owner of the Charlotte Hornets, George Shinn. Shinn had brought the NBA to the city and wanted to expand his sports empire with a Minor League baseball team. Shinn was living in Charlotte at the time, and would eventually settle in Tega Cay, a lakefront town adjacent to Fort Mill. He hailed from Kannapolis, North Carolina, yet another textile town not unlike Fort Mill. He had worked in the mill there and gone on to make his fortune. Bayles liked that he had come from humble origins. "I think anybody who pulls themselves up by their bootstraps and really makes it is okay," he said.

Baseball wasn't a new idea for Charlotte. The city had been home to the Charlotte Orioles until their stadium burned and the team owner opted not to continue. Shinn wanted to start a new team that would be a Double A program affiliated with the Chicago Cubs. But he didn't believe leaders in Charlotte would help him see it through. Additionally, he had hoped to eventually expand to an NFL franchise as well. This was before Jerry Richardson successfully landed the Panthers. Shinn hoped to build a stadium facility that could serve both baseball and football. A football stadium would have to have much greater seating capacity. At the time, 40,000 was considered a reasonable number. But Shinn believed that to support an NFL team, he would need South Carolina in the mix.

Bayles explained the reason for Shinn's thinking on that subject.

"North Carolina was a basketball state and South Carolina was a football state."

Even so, Bayles and Shinn approached the City of Charlotte with the venture and were turned down.

With a South Carolina location in mind, Bayles went to work finding one. A local couple who were clients of his, Doyle and Nancy Jennings, owned significant property in Fort Mill near I-77. He was able to broker a deal in which the owners would give thirty-two acres to the county for the stadium to be built. At the same time, Shinn would pay them $1 million for the donated land that the county would then own. The deal was struck and the next step was coming up with the perfect stadium design to meet the immediate needs of a baseball team and the future needs of a potential football franchise.

The former owner of the Charlotte Oriels, Frances Crockett, lent her private plane so Bayles and Shinn could travel across the country touring stadiums. They visited Buffalo, New York; Richmond, Virginia; Columbus, Ohio; and Hoover, Alabama, among several others. A design was finalized that allowed for a baseball stadium that could seat 10,000 fans with expansion capability to 40,000 if the football plan came to fruition.

Shinn built his stadium on land brokered by Bayles and the Charlotte Knights played ball there for twenty-four years. Today the team is a Triple A affiliate for the Chicago White Sox, and they play at a new stadium in Uptown Charlotte. With Jerry Richardson's Carolina Panthers in the NFL slot, Shinn continued to focus on his NBA Hornets franchise, which had been established in 1988. In the early 2000s after an ugly, protracted battle with city officials over a new arena for the team, Shinn moved the franchise to New Orleans. The feud left a bitter taste in the mouths of a lot of local residents and Shinn's reputation suffered. But Bayles remembered the tenacious former mill town boy who had brought high-profile sports to a city that had none at all when he began. "He is a fine fellow. I don't care what people say about him. He was aggressive, yes, an aggressive businessman, but he was a good businessman. He knew how to make things happen. People get mad at people who can make things happen."

Closer to home, Bayles worked with the York County Economic Development Council on incentives like "Fee in Lieu" that helped attract businesses by allowing them to pay a tax fee in lieu of regular assessed taxes. When Bayles had been chairman of the York County Council, he, along with Baxter Hood and Gene Klugh had created the economic development group and had gotten it approved by the larger county council. He also served on the county's Strategic Planning Commission and also on the Rock Hill–Fort Mill Area Transportation Study (RFATS), a group that plans for transportation projects and sets infrastructure priorities.

In the 1980s Bayles and friend Harry Hogue, York County assessor, started an organization called the Businessmen's Association of York County with the purpose of working behind the scenes on issues that needed government attention. Bayles was its first president and Hogue was secretary/treasurer. Johnny Neal would come on board in the early 90s. Before long they had ninety influential area leaders involved.

Hogue described the venture: "The breakdown was to get businessmen throughout York County who would get involved in issues that were taking place. At that time the big issue was Water West. It's always been a controversy of East vs. West in York County. East, being Rock Hill, controlled everything because they had the source of water. West would be anything past Newport going westward, including York, Clover, Hickory Grove, Sharon, and so on. We didn't have countywide water. York had their own water system, but it wasn't a great system and they wanted countywide water. So that was the first big issue and we started getting members from Fort Mill, Rock Hill, Clover, York, and Hickory Grove into this association and we would talk about issues and try to bring them to the front to county government as well as local government and bring in speakers at our retreats. We did the retreats at Myrtle Beach once a year. It [the group] still exists but it's not as big as it used to be and probably not as functional as it used to be. Bayles would help us in his capacity as highway commissioner. We'd talk about getting roads paved; just different issues in the background. We never were out front. Eventually it has worked out well because the East and West have gotten along better."

Since 1990 Bayles has served on the Business and Industry Political Education Committee (BIPEC) for South Carolina. The organization evaluates members of the state legislature and publishes scorecards based on how they vote on business-related issues. It began as part of the state chamber of commerce but ultimately became its own entity. BIPEC has a director who lobbies for business and industry. The group conducts research on the population and demographics of each district and whether the population of that district votes pro-business or not. BIPEC rates both the district and its representative. If a legislator gets a 100-percent rating by voting pro-business for an entire year, he or she is awarded a sword and mace.

As the years went by, Bayles found himself pulled in different directions by commitments to his law practice, business dealings, political efforts, and the myriad of organizations he supported. With multiple plates spinning, something was bound to give. Despite professional success and an outward appearance of a life that was kept in good order, there was one plate that was in danger of shattering.

HOME AND AWAY

He's my best friend.
There's nothing I can't talk to him about.

—Tina Tomlinson

Since the day Bayles saw Joanne Arnold eating her lunch behind the school, the two of them had been a matched pair. From their earliest married days furnishing their first apartment with cheap goods from across the border to the demands of life in the fishbowl that is Washington, D.C., to the unending social obligations that come with a life in the public eye, the two of them had charted a course in give-and-take that had become decidedly one-sided. Joanne was carrying the entire load at home while Bayles shook hands all around the state.

By nature, Joanne was a more private person than her husband, who seemed to collect people wherever he went. She preferred a quieter and less public life surrounded by family. Over time that family grew with the birth of seven grandchildren. Sadly, one of their granddaughters passed away unexpectedly in 2014, leaving behind not only a grieving family but also a great many friends who loved her. The Mary Warner Mack Dog Park, located in a quiet corner of the Anne Springs Close Greenway, is named in her honor.

Bayles and Joanne's children, Barry and Beth, share a similar private nature with their mother and have never sought the public spotlight of politics or the adoration of crowds. Bayles and Joanne separated in 2004 and divorced in 2011 after fifty-four years of marriage. Out of respect for their privacy, Bayles declined further comment on the family's home life except to say that despite any failings on his part, his family remains the most important part of his life.

*

It's not a secret to say Bayles was not always a faithful husband, at least not if one believed the rumors that dogged him over the years. Some were true; others were not. A man who loves to socialize and go shag dancing and has a natural charisma that attracts women is likely to be dismissed as a womanizer, but Bayles has scores of female friends with whom nothing untoward has ever happened. But then there were the others.

In the halcyon days of Bayles's early career when his law practice had taken off and he was involved in the political game at the highest level, he met a woman who would prove to be the first major challenge to his marriage. It was 1970 and the young woman—we'll call her Susan—had been hired by a political campaign colleague of Bayles's. Susan wanted to work in politics, and the secretarial job put her right in the middle of the action in Columbia. Bayles traveled to the office three days a week and over the course of several months he and Susan conducted an affair. By all accounts they had fallen hard for each other. She was engaged to a man who was in the Navy and stationed in Charleston. Despite Bayles's marital status and her upcoming marriage, she introduced Bayles to her family. From time to time she would tell Bayles that she wanted him to tell her not to marry her fiancé. Her boss and Bayles's colleague confirmed that Susan wanted to marry Bayles instead and that she hoped he would step in and prevent the upcoming marriage to the Navy man. But Bayles had a wife and two children and was not planning to leave them, and he told Susan so.

The night of the rehearsal dinner for her wedding, Susan called Bayles and asked him to come by her parents' house after the dinner ended. Bayles, a friend, and the friend's girlfriend drove to the house. Susan told Bayles she had confessed to her parents that she had been trying to get Bayles to talk her out of going through with the wedding because she wanted to marry him. She told him her parents wanted that as well. They were sitting in the back seat of a car Bayles's friend was driving when Susan's fiancé arrived. He approached the car and told Susan to get out. She refused. Ultimately she did exit the car and Bayles and his friends left. The wedding went forward the next day. Bayles, though invited, did not attend.

Throughout the years there were flirtations. Tina Tomlinson described Bayles's demeanor with women. "He is a gentleman, but in his early years he was a playboy. He didn't mind going out and carousing around," she said.

The beach was a common place of flirtation for Bayles and his love of shag dancing provided the playing field.

"He likes to dance and if he found somebody who could dance really well and was attractive he would befriend them and keep meeting them at the beach to dance but not to have a so-called affair. It was a friendship outside of being married. He just had that attraction with women because he knows how to talk," Tina explained.

Women have always been Bayles's greatest weakness. He has a deep respect for them and has actively supported equality efforts, but he also can't resist the pull of attraction. It's the dichotomy of his life. But with age comes a change in perspective—a settling down into a different phase of life. In his 60s, Bayles would finally land after a lifetime of wandering.

*

Back in 2006 when the photograph of the ribbon-cutting for Bayles's railcar office appeared in the local newspaper, an attractive woman could be seen to Bayles's left helping to hold the ribbon. She had been instrumental in getting the car ready to open, helping to plan its final décor, and managing many of the details of that event and also the ceremony where the section of I-77 had been officially named in Bayles's honor. In fact, she had been the driving force behind convincing him to accept the honor after years of putting it off. Her name is Tina Tomlinson. She was Bayles's assistant and, more importantly, the woman he came to call one of the loves of his life.

"In spite of everything, I've only had two loves in my life: Joanne and Tina," he remarked.

After opening B. Mack Mercantile, his antique store on Main Street, the need arose for someone to come in and manage the store on a daily basis. It was actually Joanne Mack who had hired Tina for that position in 1998. She had been working in the store for a short time when Bayles asked if she would consider splitting her time between the store and doing administrative work in his law office. She agreed and started working the split schedule. It didn't take long for her to figure out she didn't care much for Bayles Mack. His reputation had preceded him.

But it wasn't his reputation that bothered her personally. It was the attitude he took with her. "He was rude and I thought he was a jerk," she remembered.

After a year of tiptoeing around him, she finally told him what she thought, including how she was unimpressed by his habit of flirting with customers. Bayles and Tina recalled the scene.

"We worked together for a year and I was probably tough on her," he remembered.

"You *were* tough on me. You were rude," Tina answered.

"She couldn't stand for me to come up there [to the store]."

"I didn't like him at all. I thought he had a terrible personality. I said 'I just don't think I can work for you anymore because your personality is just so harsh. And I just don't think we get along.'"

Bayles recalled how he ran his businesses and could see some validity in her comments. "Well, I governed my work by fear sometimes," he admitted.

Nothing changed right away, but as they worked together more over the next couple of months it seemed to dawn on Bayles that Tina had not been far off in her estimation.

"It sunk in that I should be better about it," he said.

"He didn't realize he was being rude," she remembered. Bayles explained that his curt treatment of her was just part of his tendency to be somewhat hard on staff who worked for him. Despite his personable demeanor when he's charming a potential political donor or asking for a dance at the beach pavilion, in his business dealings he's a workaholic and a demanding boss. Nonetheless, he recognized that he had offended her, and his efforts to be more sensitive in his communication with her led to an improvement in their professional relationship.

Looking back on the things she had heard about his reputation around town as a rich lawyer and money-man type, over the years Tina developed an opinion about how that reputation came to be. "People think he has a lot of money, but he has a lot of *things*, property, and so on. He's not the rich, wealthy man people think he is. He has lots of holdings, but he still borrows money to make investments. He'll make an investment, then pay it off, then borrow some more and make another investment. That's what makes him tick. It doesn't worry him; he's very positive minded. He's looking for the next thing to do. He gets bored and likes to change things. He loves change. He's eight-five and still thinks ahead twenty years."

As their professional relationship improved with Bayles's efforts at kinder interactions, things began to take a turn between them on a personal level. It was 1998. Bayles had an interest in antiques and enjoyed the hunt for unique pieces, especially those with a known history, so it was not uncommon for him to work in the store on Saturdays when he had the time. One particular Saturday he was helping Tina change lightbulbs upstairs. When she stepped off the ladder he kissed her. She remembered being very nervous. He was a married man and his wife had been the person to give her the job in the store. To complicate matters further, Tina was also married.

"I never set out to do anything wrong. I did not," Tina said.

Bayles concurred, "Neither one of us did."

"It grew into a real love and a true, real friendship," she recalled.

Fort Mill is a small town and people talk. It wasn't the first rumor to go around about Bayles and a woman who was not his wife. Further inflaming the gossip grapevine, Tina is thirty years younger than Bayles.

Still, no one came out and asked questions about their relationship publicly. Tina admits, "It was known but not acknowledged."

Bayles wanted to make Tina a partner in the store. Her involvement had grown beyond simply managing the retail portion. She was active in purchasing as well, and she showed a natural talent for home décor and design that proved to be a benefit to the store's bottom line. She wanted to buy in and become a co-owner, and they worked out a deal that allowed her to increase her stock percentage over the course of three years until she had control of 50 percent of the company.

Bayles and Tina went on buying trips for their store and also for a successful local auction house that operated out of another building Bayles owned on Main Street. They each had an excellent eye for antiques and their business continued to grow. The auction house ceased operations, but work continued at the store until Tina suffered health issues that forced her to take considerable time away from the business.

Bayles credits Tina's involvement in not only the store but also in his other businesses as well, stating, "Every decision made after 2004 by me, she was involved with."

Tina credits Bayles with teaching her skills that have helped her in her career, not only as a store owner but also in her role as his assistant where she had interaction with state agencies and legal clients.

"I'm not saying he changed me, but he showed me the proper way to be and the proper way to act—the proper Southern way. I wasn't like that. I was so young and naïve when I first went to work for him. I didn't know how to act. He taught me how to behave in a professional setting, how to dress and wear my hair." He also bought her a professional wardrobe, everything she needed to put her best foot forward.

Things were not always rosy in their personal relationship, given Bayles's knack for flirtation. Tina had been intricately involved in the planning of the ceremony for the naming of a section of I-77 for Bayles and things came to a head that night. A friend of Bayles's, who was a known playboy, had arrived at the ceremony with a woman Bayles had known from the DOT in Columbia. Tina served as greeter for the guests, making sure everyone had nametags and programs. It kept her tethered to one spot near the door so she could watch the festivities only from that vantage point. What she saw was an infuriating show with the intoxicated woman dancing with Bayles and the two of them partying hard.

"She was all over him—*all* over him. And *he* was all over *her*," Tina said in describing the scene.

Eventually Tina had had enough and the event was coming to an end, so she grabbed her best friend, Sally, and they left. "I said to heck with it and we decided we were going to go dance somewhere. That wasn't a place we wanted to be anymore," she remembered.

The women went to the Holiday Inn on Woodlawn in Charlotte, a regular gathering spot with a band and dancing. When Bayles found out she had left, he and some friends went looking for her. Bayles knew the Holiday Inn was a good place to check, and they arrived there to find several Fort Mill friends who reported that Tina and Sally had been there and had just left.

Bayles and his friends went back to the house Bayles had moved into during the separation from Joanne, and Tina and Sally stopped by shortly thereafter. When Tina realized the woman from the ceremony party was present, she and Sally left for Sally's house.

The woman had indeed been at the house, but she was there with her date, not with Bayles. Both Bayles and Tina believe the man, a friend of Bayles's, had instigated the whole scene. Bayles and Johnny Neal went to Sally's house and Tina and Bayles were able to resolve their conflict that night.

Despite the occasional disagreements, Tina is quick to focus on the strength of the relationship itself.

"He's a proper Southern gentleman and I can say that because of the way he treated me. Bayles is different when he's around a crowd than when he's just with me. He's very subdued when he's with me. He always made sure that I'm okay, that I'm all right. If I'm upset, he sits down and listens. He's a good listener and he gives great advice. I can't say anything but good things about him. I mean, he has a sordid past; I know he does." But Tina lets that past lie where it rests.

"We've been together a long time and we've gotten very close. He's my best friend. He's the love of my life. He really is. I've never cared about anybody the way I've cared about him. I don't think of him being older than me. I know he is, but none of that bothers me. I enjoy helping him. It's because I love him."

She adds, "He's helped me through a lot of different personal situations that have been difficult, and he's been my best friend. He tells me the same thing."

Tina does worry sometimes about what others may think of her and how people may view their age difference as an indication that she is out for financial gain. She stresses that she does not expect to be and does not aspire to be included in any inheritance. She says her only financial interest is the store.

"I don't want anything. He and I are partners in the store and that's all I care about—our partnership in the store. Other than that, I just care about him. I love Bayles."

THE GROWN-UP BOYS' CLUB

It was hard to call him "Mr. Mack" in the office.

—Johnny Neal

We've called him worse than that.

—Harry Hogue

Just as in the summer days between school years when Bayles would spend weeks at the beach with his family and best friends, he continues to cherish his time there and shares it frequently with friends he met during the course of his adult life.

Johnny Neal was two years ahead of Bayles at Fort Mill High. Neal forged a career in the military, and after retirement he returned to

Fort Mill and took a job working with Bayles while he was on the highway commission.

"I was kind of his 'go-fer' at the highway department."

Harry Hogue became friends with Bayles in 1961 when the Jaycees started a chapter in Clover. Three months later, a Fort Mill chapter was formed and Bayles was its first president. In his role as county tax assessor, Hogue had known Bayles previously from his frequent trips to the old courthouse to research abstracts for property transfers. When Bayles became chairman of the county council, he was in effect Hogue's boss. They were both active in Jaycees.

Jack Windell rounded out the group when he returned with his wife to her hometown of Fort Mill and moved into the house next door to the Macks in 1971. Windell was the human resources manager for Springs Industries for thirty-five years. After his retirement in 2005, he worked for Bayles one year on a project for the highway commission until funding for it was cut.

Eventually all three men would work for Bayles in some capacity, but it was their friendship that brought them together to talk about the man they know and to tell stories about their exploits to Myrtle Beach—adventures that continue to this day.

Johnny Neal and Bayles both have September birthdays, so the group travels to the beach to celebrate them. September falls right at the height of hurricane season, and in 2018 their trip was cut short by Hurricane Florence. But even without a natural disaster, the men like to stir things up on their annual trip.

If there's not a hurricane in a given year, "we make one," boasts Hogue.

Johnny Neal tells a story of a time before Bayles had a house at the beach. The two of them headed down for the annual meeting of the state Jaycees without arranging for a place to stay. They were out of luck when they got there, as rooms were scarce. The Jaycees were holding their retreat at the famous Ocean Forest Hotel. When Bayles and Neal arrived at 2:00 a.m., the party was going strong outside the hotel. The group had put together a miniature "train" made up of lawnmowers complete with a whistle that blew. The participants had been drinking heavily and the police had already been by to tell the revelers that if that train was seen one more time, they would start locking people up. Undeterred, Bayles and Neal hopped on for a ride, blowing the whistle and having a grand time. After the train ride, someone from the group had commandeered a ladder and Bayles attempted to climb the outside of the hotel on it. Finally, the two men got back into the car and started driving around.

"I'm going to buy a house down here," Bayles announced.

On their drive they spotted a little yellow house with a "for sale" sign and Bayles said he would buy that one.

"Sure enough, he did. He bought it," Neal said.

In later years Bayles would sell that house and build the one in Ocean Drive where he still vacations today. The three men described what they do when they go to the beach and it involves a lot of drinking and shag dancing.

Neal reported, "We just go dancing and sit around drinking and eating."

"No, we don't eat anything," Windell contradicted. "The first time I went down there with them I nearly starved to death."

Hogue laughed, remembering Windell's first trip. "I remember Jack saying, 'When we gonna eat?'" There was just too much drinking and dancing going on for the others to be thinking about eating.

Another favorite pastime is sitting on the front porch at the house in Ocean Drive and asking questions of "the answer man."

"Bayles is 'the answer man,'" Neal explained.

Hogue chimed in: "You can ask him any question and he's got an answer, but you might not like it! 'What time is the moon coming out?' He doesn't hesitate. He'll tell you right quick an answer, but it might not make sense."

Neal says that if you ask him any question about the law, his answer will always be "You got a witness?"

On another occasion when Neal and Hogue were working for Bayles at the Mack and Mack office, Bayles sent them to Myrtle Beach to handle a meeting involving a highway project.

Harry told him, "We don't know a damn thing about that highway."

Bayles said, "Act like you do."

"So we kicked a little dirt and went to a meeting at their headquarters. The company called later and said we did a good job!"

Neal revealed an ongoing joke they will not let go of regarding their not receiving any per diem for the trip. Every time they go to the beach they needle Bayles about it. "We never did get our per diem," they remind him.

Bayles's response is always the same: "Did y'all spend the night in my house?"

"Yeah."

"Then your per diem is gone!"

The men revel in their ongoing rebuke. While they all laugh, Neal reiterates, "Every time we go down there we mention it. We sit out on the porch drinking and we say, 'By the way Bayles, we know they paid it but we didn't get it!'"

There is a lot of laughter at the table where the men are reminiscing, but they are quick to talk about Bayles's kindness as well. He came to the aid of Hogue's son for his law school admission.

"He helped get my son in law school with his political connections. He had graduated from South Carolina, but they had turned him down and he had to go to Michigan for one year. I told Bayles. He made a call, telling his contact, 'He [Hogue's son] is a graduate of South Carolina. It looks like he ought to be able to get into the law school.' Two weeks later he got notification that they had accepted him.'"

At the end of their time together, after a great deal of laughter, both at themselves and at Bayles, Johnny Neal makes a remark that stirs up the revelry again.

"We could sit here for three days and tell you about stuff," he tells me.

Harry Hogue chimes in: "But you couldn't put it in the book! That would ruin you—and him!"

"And us! Especially us!" That's Jack Windell. Almost like it was scripted, the men pop off with their comedic lines, cracking each other up in the process. This is a tight group of friends who have spent a lot of time together. Add in the fourth man, the ringleader, and it's not surprising if it seems there *is* a hurricane at Myrtle Beach every September.

A LIFE AND A
LEGACY

---

*You can't do anything about the length of your life, but
you can do something about its width and depth.*

—H.L. Mencken

Bayles Mack's railcar office is a microcosm of his world, of his time on
the planet. If awards and commendations are proof of a productive
existence, then the walls of the railcar hold all the proof anyone would
need. But they are not the measure of a life.

Interspersed among the accolades are framed photos and
memorabilia that speak to connections with important people and
highly visible achievements. But these are not the basis of a life well
lived either.

Of course it's wonderful to be recognized for one's hard work and to be lauded by one's peers. But the evidence of such is not an adequate reward at the end of the journey. But if you look closely among these things, there is evidence of greater value.

An original leather-bound, two-volume set of his grandfather's legal books.

The stripes and bars from his military uniform.

His mother's name emblazoned down the side of the car in tribute.

And then there are the people. Not the ones of mere acquaintance met in passing in pursuit of political gains or the ones who judge from a distance.

The lifelong friends who remember a simpler, better era and the boy who drove them around in his father's Studebaker.

The colleagues who knew how the game was played and yet recognized a square-dealer when they saw one.

The shag dancers at the pavilion by the beach.

This is where you will find the jewels of Bayles's legacy.

"Bayles is far from the norm. He's not afraid to take a risk. He wants to be different and he doesn't care if everyone likes him." —Tina Tomlinson

"He was my best friend growing up and I have a great appreciation for how he brought me out of the mill hill. He introduced me to another kind of life." —Regi Thackston

"He was a peacemaker. He would make sure the issue was resolved and he always sought the common ground." —Betty Mabry

"Never to my knowledge has he ever tried to draw any social lines between himself and average common people." —Don Fowler

"He's been somewhat the quintessential small town lawyer who has transitioned because of his personality into a statewide network—a network throughout the Carolinas really because his influence extends very much into North Carolina. His personality is an infectious personality. People just like to be around him. —John Napier

"I think Dad's legacy will be his civic accomplishments. And he loves his family. It's very important to him." —Beth Mack Reigel

"If he's a friend of yours he's a friend for life, even if he can make you madder than hell!" —Harry Hogue

*

In reality, to understand the real legacy of Bayles Mack, the one he himself wants to leave, you have to take a trip to the beach. In the house in Ocean Drive, his legacy is on display in full color. It is a life-size mural he had commissioned of his family. They are Bayles Mack's legacy.

But the man who has spent years and years keeping all the plates spinning is not ready to give it up just yet.

"People may think I should quit. But I feel like I can still do some good." As long as there is good to be done and beach music for dancing, Libba Mack's only son plans to keep on spinning.

BARRON BAYLES
MACK

List of Affiliations and Commendations

EDUCATION
- B.S in Political Science, Davidson College, 1956
- Juris Doctor, Washington and Lee University, 1960
- Sigma Phi Epsilon Social Fraternity
- President, Epsilon Chapter, Davidson College, 1956
- President, Virginia Epsilon Chapter, Washington and Lee University, 1958
- President, Phi Delta Phi Legal Fraternity, 1959

POLITITCS AND GOVERNMENT
- Executive Committeeman, York County Democratic Party, 1964–1965
- Executive Committee, State Democratic Party for York County, 1972–1996

- Administrative Assistant to Congressman Tom S. Gettys, South Carolina 5th District, 1966–1970
- Delegate to Democratic National Convention, 1968, 1972
- Magistrate, Fort Mill Township, York County, 1969–1970
- Town Attorney, Town of Fort Mill, 1969–2013
- Member of SC Legislative Crime Committee, appointed by Gov. John C. West, 1971–1975
- York County Election Commission, 1974–1975
- Councilman and Chairman, York County Council, two terms
- Member and Chairman, York County Economic Development Board
- South Carolina Educational Television Commission, 1983–1987
- SC Dept. of Transportation Commissioner, 5th Congressional Dist. 1979-1981, 1987-1991, 1994-1996, 2000-2004.

BUSINESS AND PROFESSIONAL

- Partner, Mack and Mack Attorneys-at-Law, 1960-present
- Member, South Carolina Bar
- Member, York County Bar
- Member, American Trial Lawyers
- Owner, B. Mack Mercantile
- Owner, Rugs and Antiques 1981-present
- Owner, Market on Main
- President/Treasurer, Mack Title Insurance Agency
- Member/Manager, B. Mack and Co. Real Estate, Myrtle Beach, SC
- Chairman/Treasurer, York County Growth Partners

- Chairman, Carolinas Partnership (Charlotte USA) Board of Directors, 1997-1998. Member 1989-present.
- President, Fort Mill Chamber of Commerce, 1963
- Member, Charlotte Douglas International Airport Commission, 1995-1996
- Chairman, Rock Hill Chamber of Commerce, 1995-1996
- Chairman, South Carolina Advisory Board, Wells Fargo
- President, Fort Mill Jaycees 1961-1962
- Distinguished Service Award & Outstanding Young Man of the Year, Fort Mill Jaycees 1962
- Citizen of the Year, Fort Mill Area Chamber of Commerce, 1999
- Member/Judge Advocate/Historian, American Legion Post 43, 63 years
- Member/Manager, Living Legends of O.D. and Grand Strand, LLC, North Myrtle Beach, SC (shag dancing organization
- Member/Manager, Downtown Partners, LLC, Fort Mill

MILITARY SERVICE
- Second Lieutenant, US. Army Anti-Aircraft Artillery, 1956
- Judge Advocates General Corps
- Honorable Discharge, rank of Captain, 1968
- Re-entered service, SC National Guard, 2001
- Rank, Lieutenant Colonel
- Rank, Colonel, Joint Services Detachment, SC National Guard
- Board of Directors, ESGR, State of SC, (Employer support of the Guard & Reserve)

RELIGIOUS AFFILIATION

- Member, Unity Presbyterian Church, Fort Mill
- Deacon/Elder, Unity Presbyterian Church, Fort Mill
- President, Men of the Church, Unity Presbyterian Church, Fort Mill
- Sunday School Teacher, Unity Presbyterian Church, Fort Mill
- Oldest Member, Unity Presbyterian Church, Fort Mill, 2021

AUTHOR'S NOTES

Many people contributed to this project, sharing their time and their treasured memories. It wouldn't have been possible without the gracious participation of the late Don Fowler, Harry Hogue, John Neal, Jack Windell, Betty Mabry, Jim Howie, Gigi Mills Poole, Gene Ervin, David Hudspeth, Tina Tomlinson, Regi Thackston, and Beth Reigel. I'm very appreciative to my early readers, Joel Hamilton and Judge John L. Napier, and also to Judge Napier for his support in writing the foreword for the book. Research was conducted with the help of the South Carolina Department of Archives and History, the York County Library, the South Caroliniana Library, the South Carolina Political Collections department of the University of South Carolina Library, and the York County Sheriff's Department. The book in your hands owes its final polish to the painstaking proofreading of Jonathan Wright and the cover and interior layout design of Mark Thomas.

Of course, my greatest thanks go to Bayles Mack himself for trusting me with his life story. I met Bayles seven years ago when I interviewed him for a video project about the history of Fort Mill. Since that time,

I have found him to be a most interesting, knowledgeable, and truly kind man. I wish I could say this book captures all there is to know about Bayles, but that would be a departure from the truth. There is a vast network of people, places, and events that live in his memory, and he continues to make new connections every day. Whether it's a chance meeting of town newcomers at his favorite local restaurant or a call from a friend of a friend looking for his unique take on a particular political race, Bayles treats every day like a new adventure and loves to see what he can get into. I can only hope to have the longevity and zest for life that he shows day in and day out. If you have a chance to pop into Hobo's on Main Street in Fort Mill and catch a glimpse of the gentleman holding court with a group of people around him, I hope you'll take a moment to introduce yourself. It will be an experience that will bring something special into your life as it has in mine.

—*LeAnne Burnett Morse*

NOTES

1 "I have a splendid place here...section is growing": Joseph Bingham Mack to his father, William Mack. 1876. *Mack Family Papers*, South Caroliniana Library, p. 87.

2 "I feel that God sent me...sign to leave or not?": Joseph Bingham Mack to his father, William Mack. 1876. *Mack Family Papers*, South Caroliniana Library, p. 87.

3 "[I] hoped things would be permanent...Lord be with you.": Letter from William Mack to son Joseph Bingham Mack, April 20, 1876. *Mack Family Papers*, South Caroliniana Library, p. 88.

4 "I am getting old...suddenly happen to Your Father.": Letter from Joseph Bingham Mack to son William Mack, August 15, 1899. Personal collection of B. Bayles Mack.

5 "has been put on foot...Broadway, New York.": *The American Lawyer*, November, 1900. Stumpf & Steuer, p. 499.

6 "the work will not be done by...under his direction.": *The American Lawyer*, November, 1900. Stumpf & Steuer, p. 499.

7 To Charles Walter Dumont...dedicated to him. Dedication by William Mack to Charles Dumont. *Cyclopedia of Law and Procedure, Volume XL*, April, 1912, The American Law Book Company, New York

8   "...who was born just three years prior." Bayles Shipyard records. August 22, 2017. http://shipbuildinghistory.com/shipyards/19thcentury/bayles.htm

9   "Your old-fashioned ideas...Southern school.": Letter from William Mack to his mother Harriet Banks Mack, March 1, 1891. *Mack Family Papers*, South Caroliniana Library, p. 129.

10   "I am not surprised...disturbing the community.": Letter from William Mack Sr. to William Mack Jr. (Billee), June 21, 1937. Personal collection of B. Bayles Mack.

11   "I wish Bayles had Roma's...a good possum dog.": Letter (1 of 2) from William Mack Sr. to William Mack Jr. (Billee), October 11, 1937. Personal collection of B. Bayles Mack

12   "Am glad to hear...mother was a Baptist." Letter (2 of 2) from William Mack Sr. to William Mack Jr. (Billee), October 11, 1937. Personal collection of B. Bayles Mack.

13   "Tell Elizabeth...Christmas present.": Letter from William Mack Sr. to William Mack Jr. (Billee), August 19, 1938. Personal collection of B. Bayles Mack

14   "Be sure to see that...by this instrument.": Letter from William Mack Sr. to Mrs. W.B. Mack, June 1, 1939. Personal collection of B. Bayles Mack

15   William Mack Jr. (Billee), April 26, 1939. Personal collection of B. Bayles Mack.

16   "Tell him [Bayles]...in on our country.": Letter from William Mack Sr. to William Mack Jr. (Billee), September 22, 1939. Personal collection of B. Bayles Mack

17   "This being a Republican...other Northern Folks.": Letter from William Mack Sr. to William Mack Jr. (Billee), December 31, 1937. Personal collection of B. Bayles Mack

18   "This is St. Patrick's Day...an acre in 1939.": Letter from William Mack Sr. to William Mack Jr. (Billee), March 17, 1939. Personal collection of B. Bayles Mack.

19   "Glad to know you are...decisions of your state.": Letter from William Mack Sr. to William Mack Jr. (Billee), June 21, 1937. Personal collection of B. Bayles Mack.

20   "A letter from Uncle Ed...from all the heirs...": Letter from William Mack Sr. to William Mack Jr. (Billee), September 13, 1937. Personal collection of B. Bayles Mack

21   William Mack Jr. (Billee), October 5, 1937. Personal collection of B. Bayles Mack.

22 "P.S. Have not heard…make other arrangements.": Letter from William Mack Sr. to Mrs. W.B. Mack, October 8, 1937. Personal collection of B. Bayles Mack.

23 "I have been wholly willing…transaction is consummated.": Letter (1 of 2) from William Mack Sr. to William Mack Jr. (Billee), October 11, 1937. Personal collection of B. Bayles Mack.

24 "As I have not heard…cancel your authority.": Letter (2 of 2) from William Mack Sr. to William Mack Jr. (Billee), October 11, 1937. Personal collection of B. Bayles Mack.

25 "It is difficult to see…handled this job.": Letter (1 of 2) from William Mack Sr. to William Mack Jr. (Billee), October 19, 1937. Personal collection of B. Bayles Mack.

26 "Tomorrow will be your…Devotedly, Dad.": Letter (2 of 2) from William Mack Sr. to William Mack Jr. (Billee), October 19, 1937. Personal collection of B. Bayles Mack.

27 "The defendant's fiancé…all day Sunday.": *The Evening Herald,* Rock Hill, South Carolina, December 11, 1948, p.5

28 Supreme Court of South Carolina, *Mickle v. Blackmon,Mssrs. James P. Mozingo, III, and D. Kenneth Baker, of Darlington Hayes, Brunson & Gatlin, of Rock Hill, William E. Chandler, of Greenville, and Greer and Chandler, of Darlington, for Appellant, Janet Mickle.* February 10, 1969. Leagle.com, https://www.leagle.com/decision/1969454252sc2021435, Accessed January 10, 2018

29 "In all honesty, in real trouble in South Carolina this year." Letter from Lachlan L. Hyatt to Governor Robert E. McNair, September 23, 1968. South Carolina Political Collections Library, University of South Carolina

30 "Like anybody I…to the Promised Land.": *I've Been to the Mountaintop,* Speech by Dr. Martin Luther King, Jr. to striking sanitation workers, Memphis, Tennessee, April 3, 1968.

31 "America is the black man's battleground.": Protesters shouting at Selective Service Director, General Lewis B. Hershey, March 1967. Washington Post, *What Happened to the Howard Class of '68?,* Jacqueline Trescott and Paul Henderson, May 15, 1978. https://www.washingtonpost.com/archive/lifestyle/1978/05/15/what-happened-to-the-howard-class-of-68/d4db6769-0d81-4366-8cd3-225f3042cee4/

32   "My thanks to all of you…let's win there.": *Speech to Democratic Supporters at the Ambassador Hotel, Los Angeles*, California, Robert F. Kennedy, June 5, 1968.

33   "The [South Carolina] delegation shall on all issues cast their vote under the unit rule." *Resolution to be Submitted to the South Carolina Democratic Convention by the Resolution Committee Dealing with the Method of Selecting Delegates to the National Democratic Convention.*: Adopted March 28, 1968. South Carolina Political Collections Library, University of South Carolina.

34   "A copy of the state party's resolution…addition in the meeting." *Resolution to be Submitted to the South Carolina Democratic Convention by the Resolution Committee Dealing with the Method of Selecting Delegates to the National Democratic Convention.*: Adopted March 28, 1968. South Carolina Political Collections Library, University of South Carolina.

35   Itemized invoice from Schedule A and Schedule B: Letter from Frank Hogan to Don Fowler. August 21, 1968. South Carolina Political Collections Library, University of South Carolina.

36   "The South Carolina party is now in the mainstream." *South Carolina Democrats United with National Party*: Rock Hill Evening Herald, Lee Bandy, August 24, 1968.

37   "…the draft movement has gone too far to be stopped." *Convention is on: Kennedy Rebuffs Draft Movement*: Special to the New York Times, Tom Wicker, August 28, 1968.

38   "…could avoid what could be a disastrous year for the Democrats." *Convention is on: Kennedy Rebuffs Draft Movement*: Special to the New York Times, Tom Wicker, August 28, 1968.

39   "There is no Southern bloc." Robert McNair to convention delegates. Rock Hill Evening Herald, Chicago AP, August 27, 1968.

40   "I don't mind the people of York County…Hubert Humphrey." Bayles Mack to reporter, *State Reaction Cool*, Rock Hill Evening Herald, August 29, 1968.

41   *Sons of South Saved HHH*, Beacon Journal-Chicago Daily News, William McGaffin, August 30, 1968

42   "We are proud of SC delegations dignity…you on the ticket." Western Union

Telegram from Anne and Jim Berry of Marion, South Carolina, August 29, 1968. South Carolina Political Collections Library, University of South Carolina.

43 "When I went to bed at 5 o'clock...for the second spot." *State Reaction Cool,* Bayles Mack to Rock Hill Evening Herald, August 29, 1968.

44 "I personally appreciate your willingness...locking up the convention." Letter from Robert E. McNair to William J. Bryan Dorn, September 5, 1968. South Carolina Political Collections Library, University of South Carolina.

45 "In the final analysis...from the South on the ticket." Letter from Robert E. McNair to R.B. Pamplin, September 6, 1968. South Carolina Political Collections Library, University of South Carolina.

46 "In keeping with the call from...I am sorry it didn't bear fruit." Letter from R.B. Pamplin to Robert E. McNair, September 6, 1968. South Carolina Political Collections Library, University of South Carolina

47 "...for it affects many South Carolinians...or its platform." Letter from Donald G. Coker to Robert E. McNair, September 10, 1968. South Carolina Political Collections Library, University of South Carolina.

48 "I appreciate your most complimentary letter...impression of us to the people of South Carolina." Letter from Robert E. McNair to James J. Reid, September 20, 1968. South Carolina Political Collections Library, University of South Carolina.

49 "It was a memorable experience. If you are ever...come by to see me." Letter from Bayles Mack to Robert E. McNair, September 9, 1968. South Carolina Political Collections Library, University of South Carolina.

50 "defined in any kind of degree...is paramount." "If the uncertainties involved... The damn country can't stand four more years of Nixon." Letter from Donald Fowler to Lawrence F. O'Brien, May 1, 1972. South Carolina Political Collections Library, University of South Carolina

51 "If we lost they'd blame me. Then you'd never hear the end of it." *The New York Post,* Edward Kennedy to Joseph Kraft, May 6, 1972.

52 "There ought to be at least...era of my brothers." *The New York Post,* Edward Kennedy to Joseph Kraft, May 6, 1972.

53 "I happen to disagree with Kraft...to be used to stop the White Knight." Letter

from William F. Haddad to Robert E. McNair, May 9, 1972. South Carolina Political Collections Library, University of South Carolina.

54   "...relatively small group of Southern delegates...formulation of a Southern coalition." Letter from Howard M. Lee to Robert E. McNair, July 10, 1972. South Carolina Political Collections Library, University of South Carolina.

55   "What kind of loserism had afflicted them?" Germaine Greer reacting to failure of feminist activists to push for inclusion of party platform plank. New York Times, July 1972.

56   "To say the least...we should have won." Letter from Hubert H. Humphrey to Robert E. McNair, July 14, 1972. South Carolina Political Collections Library, University of South Carolina.

57   "I still can't believe the whole thing...how did it happen?" Letter from Kenneth E. Calender to Robert E. McNair, July 26, 1972. South Carolina Political Collections Library, University of South Carolina

58   "Would you believe things have gotten worse." Letter from Robert E. McNair to Kenneth E. Calender, August 2, 1972. South Carolina Political Collections Library, University of South Carolina

59   "Although you attracted a lot of attention...if we had nominated him." Letter from Robert E. McNair to C.D. Sexton, August 2, 1972. South Carolina Political Collections Library, University of South Carolina

60   "...he made an effort to get home on time." Incident Follow Up Report, Statement of Terry Gerald, November 24, 1982, York County Sheriff's Department Case File.

61   "Buddy and Shirley had taken it for a drive   running properly" Incident Follow Up Report, Statement of Jerri Lynn Gerald, November 23, 1982, York County Sheriff's Department Case File.

62   "She relayed to Rister...all the time." Incident Follow Up Report, Statement of Teresa Rister, November 30, 1982, York County Sheriff's Department Case File.

63   "She had told him to get off his tail and go get gas and cut the grass." Incident Follow Up Report, Statement of Teresa Rister, November 30, 1982, York County Sheriff's Department Case File.

64   "...Terry left the house to drive Rister home." Incident Follow Up Report, Statement of Teresa Rister, November 30, 1982, York County Sheriff's Department Case File.

65   "Lynne played cards while her...then she went to bed." Incident Follow Up Report, Statement of Jerri Lynne Gerald, November 23, 1982, York County Sheriff's Department Case File.

66   "She told him Lynne had arrived home...Monte Carlo on the side of Steele Street...on Saturday morning." Incident Follow Up Report, Statement of Ladd Mills, November 22, 1982, York County Sheriff's Department Case File.

67   "As officers from the sheriff's department...noted their impressions." Mills Murder typed narrative, November 21, 1982. York County Sheriff's Department Case File.

68   "Both doors were unlocked but shut. The driver's side window was down about ten inches." Mills Murder typed narrative, November 21, 1982. York County Sheriff's Department Case File.

69   "There was an area of blood...also smeared across the passenger seat." Mills Murder typed narrative, November 21, 1982. York County Sheriff's Department Case File.

70   "Another report...may have continued moving several yards." Mills Murder typed narrative, November 21, 1982. York County Sheriff's Department Case File.

71   "An inventory lists...used for mixed drinks." List of Personal Property Recovered from the Body of Gilbert (Buddy) Mills, November 19, 1982, York County Sheriff's Department Case File.

72   "The list outlined everything Buddy had been wearing...H-ONE ROLL 35 m FILM." Autopsy Inventory and Evidence List, Lt. R.M. Jackson, November. 20, 1982, York County Sheriff's Department Case File.

73   "The final list from the autopsy...location of each." Autopsy Inventory and Evidence List, Lt. R.M. Jackson, November. 20, 1982, York County Sheriff's Department Case File.

74   *Mills Disliked Road Where He Was Killed.* Rock Hill Evening Herald, Bill McConnell, November 23, 1982

75   "She hadn't heard a call...taking a bath." Incident Follow Up Report, Statement of Shirley Mills, November 23, 1982, York County Sheriff's Department Case File.

76   "Her father had told her not to use Steele Street when she was out driving." Incident Follow Up Report, Statement of Barbara Lovett Mills "Gigi," November 24, 1982, York County Sheriff's Department Case File

77   "He responded 'yes' to a question about whether or not the crime they discussed had been carried out." Gaston County Polygraph of Donnie Carver Notes, December 29, 1982, York County Sheriff's Department Case File

78   "Stubbs told York County investigators...nothing to do with Jerry's death." Incident Follow Up Report, Statement of Coroner Bernard Stubbs, Date not listed, York County Sheriff's Department Case File.

79   "The witness said he knew it was the same car because it had a hubcap missing." Incident Follow Up Report, Statement of Chief Kimble, December 1, 1982. York County Sheriff's Department Case File.

80   "Police followed up and the lead went nowhere." Incident Follow Up Report, Statement of Julian Friday, November 25, 1982. York County Sheriff's Department Case File.

81   "...planned to kill Buddy with a shotgun." Incident Follow Up Report, Statement of Lt. Richard Jackson reporting on anonymous call, January 25, 1984, York County Sheriff's Department Case File.

82   "...brother-in-law told her he had committed a murder in Fort Mill." Follow Up Incident Report, Longview, North Carolina detective call, York County Sheriff's Department Case File.

83   "Buddy had been upset...promising shot at a new job." Follow Up Incident Report, Statement of Terry Gerald, November 24, 1982, York County Sheriff's Department Case File.

84   "It's easy for him to get depressed...in an area where gossip is constantly reminding him of Buddy." Letter from Lambert Mills to Chief Deputy W. Eugene Ervin, August 23, 1983, York County Sheriff's Department Case File.

85   "any relative correspondence...may obtain on this case." Letter from Lt. Robert
Hudgins, Criminal Investigative Division, York County Sheriff's Office, March 16,
1992, York County Sheriff's Department Case File.

ABOUT THE AUTHOR

LeAnne Burnett Morse is a native of Kentucky and a graduate of Western Kentucky University. She lives with her family in South Carolina. This is her third book.

Made in the USA
Columbia, SC
23 April 2023